Are You a Helicopter Parent?

How to Avoid the Crashes and Keep Your Parenting on Course

i

Are You a Helicopter Parent?

How to Avoid the Crashes and Keep Your Parenting on Course

Author: Pankaj Garg

Publisher: Notion Press

ISBN:

Printed in: India

Copyright @ 2024

Cover Photo & Design: Ojasvi Sharma

Dedication

To all the parents flying the parenting plane—keep your altitude, avoid turbulence, and enjoy the ride!

&

To my biggest critic and a top helicopter mom

My Wife

&

To all those who ever pestered me with their opinions unasked and unwanted

Acknowledgments

I would like to extend my heartfelt thanks to the many parents, my students, hundreds of children, and professionals who shared their experiences and insights for this book. Your stories have enriched this guide and provided invaluable perspectives. To all my esteemed colleagues at my workplace who shared their own personal experiences during parent teacher meetings and a special thanks to Dr. Vijander Singh, Ph.D. in Psychology, Faridabad, Haryana for his support and encouragement throughout this journey. Its because of all of your contributions that have been the wind beneath this book's wings!

Table of Contents

Disclaimer

This book is intended for informational purposes only and should not be considered professional advice. The insights, strategies, and examples shared are based on the author's research and experience but are not a substitute for consulting with qualified professionals, such as psychologists or parenting experts, for specific concerns.

While the author has made efforts to ensure accuracy, neither the author nor the publisher assumes any liability for any outcomes resulting from applying the content of this book. Real-life examples and case studies have been altered to protect privacy.

Readers are encouraged to use their discretion and adapt the suggestions to their unique family dynamics and needs. The content is meant to offer perspectives, not definitive solutions, and should be applied with consideration of individual circumstances.

Real-life examples and case studies have been altered to protect privacy. Any resemblance to real persons, living or dead, or actual events is purely coincidental. The use of any names, surnames, or caste references is intended for illustrative purposes only and does not imply any real-life connection or association.

The author and publisher do not intend to offend or stereotype any individual, community, or group. Any references to cultural or social identities are not meant to reflect the views or beliefs of the author or

Preface

Parenting is one of life's most profound journeys, and it's a path filled with both immense joy and complex challenges. For many of us, the instinct to protect and guide our children can sometimes evolve into a pattern of over-involvement—a phenomenon known as helicopter parenting. As a parent, you want nothing more than to see your child succeed and thrive, but in the quest for perfection and safety, it's easy to lose sight of the delicate balance between involvement and over parenting.

This book is a guide for those navigating this intricate balance. It's designed not just as a manual on helicopter parenting, but as a supportive companion for Indian parents who wish to foster a nurturing environment while empowering their children to grow into independent, confident adults.

Throughout these pages, you'll find insights into the psychology behind helicopter parenting, practical strategies for achieving a balanced approach, and real-life stories that illuminate the experiences of parents and children alike. Our aim is to provide you with a comprehensive understanding of the impacts of over parenting and offer actionable advice to help you strike a harmonious balance.

As an Indian author writing for Indian parents, I have woven cultural nuances into each chapter, acknowledging the unique challenges and expectations that shape parenting in our society. Whether you are a parent looking to make small adjustments or seeking a complete shift in approach, this book offers guidance tailored to our cultural context.

In writing this book, my goal is to empower you with knowledge and strategies that can make a meaningful difference in your parenting journey. I hope to inspire you to reflect on your own practices, embrace a more balanced approach, and ultimately, create a loving and supportive environment where your children can flourish.

As you embark on this journey through the chapters ahead, remember that parenting is not about achieving perfection but about striving for growth and understanding. It's about learning, adapting, and, above all, loving your children in a way that prepares them for the world while allowing them the freedom to discover their own paths.

Thank you for joining me on this exploration.

May you find wisdom, inspiration, and encouragement in these pages as you continue to navigate the beautiful, challenging, and rewarding journey of parenting!

Happy Parenting,

Pankaj Garg

Introduction

Taking Off

Parenting is an incredible journey—one filled with joy, challenges, and countless decisions that shape the lives of our children. In today's fast-paced, achievement-driven world, the pressure to be the perfect parent is greater than ever. We want to protect our children, guide them, and ensure they have every possible advantage. But in doing so, many of us have unintentionally found ourselves hovering a little too closely, controlling every aspect of our children's lives. This phenomenon, often referred to as "helicopter parenting," has become increasingly common, especially in India, where the stakes of education, success, and social standing feel particularly high.

But what exactly is helicopter parenting? It's when a parent becomes excessively involved in their child's life, managing even the smallest details, often out of love and concern but sometimes to the detriment of the child's independence and growth. While the intentions behind helicopter parenting are usually good, the results can be counterproductive, leading to children who are overly dependent, anxious, or ill-prepared to face the challenges of the real world.

As an Indian parent myself, I understand the cultural nuances that make helicopter parenting so prevalent in our society. Our traditions emphasize the importance of family, education, and societal reputation, often placing immense pressure on parents to ensure their children excel in every area of life. But at what cost? When does guiding turn into controlling? And how can we, as parents, find the balance between being involved and allowing our children the freedom to learn, grow, and make mistakes?

This book is not about pointing fingers or making parents feel guilty. Rather, it's about understanding the roots of helicopter parenting, recognizing its signs, and finding ways to adjust our approach to support our children's development in a healthier, more balanced way. It's about learning to land the helicopter and letting our children spread their wings.

In the chapters that follow, we'll explore the psychology behind helicopter parenting, its impact on children, and how cultural expectations play a role. We'll hear from real parents and children who have experienced the effects of over parenting, and we'll gather insights from professionals who have worked with families on these issues. Most importantly, we'll look at practical strategies for breaking the cycle, encouraging independence, and finding that delicate balance between guiding and letting go.

Whether you're a parent who's just starting to notice the signs of over involvement or someone who's been aware of it for a while and is looking for ways to change, this book is here to help. Parenting is a journey, and like any journey, it requires adjustments along the way. The good news is that it's never too late to make those adjustments, to recalibrate your approach, and to ensure that your child is equipped with the skills, confidence, and resilience they need to navigate the world on their own.

So, let's embark on this journey together. Let's explore what it means to be a helicopter parent, why we do it, and how we can find a more balanced way forward. The goal isn't to be perfect; it's to be present, mindful, and open to growth—both for ourselves and for our children.

Thank you for picking up this book. I hope it offers you the insights, encouragement, and tools you need to navigate the complexities of modern parenting with confidence and clarity.

Welcome aboard. Let's take off.

Pankaj Garg

1. Understanding Helicopter Parenting

Helicopter parenting is a term that has become widely recognized in recent years, particularly in discussions around modern parenting styles. It describes a type of parenting where parents are excessively involved in the lives of their children, often to the point of being overprotective and controlling. The term "helicopter" is used metaphorically to illustrate how these parents hover over their children, closely monitoring their activities, decisions, and interactions. The intent behind helicopter parenting is generally positive—parents want to protect their children from harm, ensure their success, and help them avoid the difficulties they themselves may have faced in life. However, this approach can have unintended consequences that affect both the child's development and the parent-child relationship.

To fully grasp the concept of helicopter parenting, it's important to consider how it differs from other parenting styles. Traditional parenting often involves setting clear boundaries and expectations while allowing children the space to learn from their own experiences. In contrast, helicopter parents may go beyond setting boundaries and instead manage or even dictate many aspects of their child's life, from what they eat and wear to the subjects they study and the friends they make. This level of involvement can prevent children from developing essential life skills such as problem-solving, decision-making, and emotional resilience.

The concept of helicopter parenting, while particularly relevant in today's context, is not entirely new. Parents have always sought to protect their children and guide them toward a successful and fulfilling life. However, in the past, this was often balanced with a recognition that children needed to learn from their own experiences, including their mistakes. In many traditional societies, including those in India, children were often given responsibilities from a young age, whether it was helping with household chores, taking care of younger siblings, or contributing to a family business. This early involvement in the practical aspects of life helped children develop a sense of responsibility and independence.

In contrast, the rise of helicopter parenting represents a shift toward a more intensive and hands-on approach, where parents take on a more active role in managing every detail of their child's life. This shift can be attributed to a variety of social, cultural, and economic factors, which we will explore in more detail in the following sections.

The Origins of Helicopter Parenting

To understand the origins of helicopter parenting, we must consider the broader social and cultural changes that have occurred over the past few decades. In India, as in many other parts of the world, the role of parents has evolved significantly, influenced by factors such as urbanization, economic growth, changing family structures, and advances in technology.

Urbanization and the Changing Role of Parents: *In the past, particularly in rural and traditional settings, the primary role of parents was to provide for the basic needs of their children—food, shelter, and education. Children were often expected to contribute to the family's livelihood, whether through agricultural work, household chores, or helping with a family business. This practical involvement in daily life naturally instilled a sense of responsibility and independence in children from a young age.*

However, with the rapid urbanization of Indian society, the dynamics of parenting have changed. In urban areas, where life is fast-paced and competitive, parents have increasingly placed a higher emphasis on their children's academic success and overall well-being. The desire to provide their children with the best possible opportunities has led parents to become more involved in their children's lives, often to the point of micromanaging every aspect of their education and development.

The Impact of Economic Growth: *Economic growth in India has brought about significant changes in the aspirations and expectations of parents. As the country has become more prosperous, the middle class has expanded, and with it, the desire for upward social mobility. Parents are now more focused on ensuring their children's success in a highly competitive job market, where a strong academic background and specialized skills are often seen as prerequisites for a stable and prosperous future.*

This focus on academic achievement has contributed to the rise of helicopter parenting, as parents feel the need to closely monitor their children's educational progress, enrol them in multiple extracurricular activities, and provide them with every possible advantage to succeed. The pressure to excel in school has become so intense that children's schedules are often packed with tutoring sessions, coaching classes, and extracurricular activities, leaving little room for unstructured play or downtime.

The Rise of Nuclear Families: *Another factor contributing to the rise of helicopter parenting is the shift from joint families to nuclear families. In traditional joint family systems, where multiple generations lived together under one roof, parenting responsibilities were often shared among various family members, including grandparents, aunts, uncles, and older siblings. This collective approach to parenting allowed children to learn from different family members and develop a broader range of social skills.*

However, as urbanization has led to the proliferation of nuclear families, parents—particularly mothers—have taken on a more central role in their children's upbringing. Without the support of extended family members, parents may feel more pressure to manage every aspect of their child's life on their own. This can lead to a more intensive and hands-on approach to parenting, where parents are constantly involved in their children's daily activities and decisions.

Cultural Expectations and the Influence of Society

In Indian society, cultural expectations play a significant role in shaping parenting behaviours. The strong emphasis on family values, respect for elders, and the importance of education deeply influences how parents raise their children. While these values have many positive aspects, they can also contribute to the pressure parents feel to ensure their children meet certain societal standards.

The Emphasis on Academic Success: *In many Indian families, academic success is seen as a key determinant of future prosperity. Parents often have high expectations for their children's academic performance, believing that excelling in school will lead to a secure and prestigious career. This emphasis on academic achievement can drive parents to become overly involved in their children's education, closely monitoring their homework, test scores, and overall progress.*

Parents may also feel pressured to enrol their children in coaching classes, tutoring sessions, and extracurricular activities to give them an edge over their peers. This intense focus on academic success can lead to a packed schedule for the child, leaving little room for free time or creative exploration. While the intention behind this involvement is to ensure the child's success, it can also create a high-pressure environment that may lead to stress, anxiety, and burnout.

The Social Pressure of "What Will People Say?" *The concept of "what will people say?" is deeply ingrained* in Indian culture. Parents are often concerned about their social standing and how their children's behaviour reflects on them within the community. This concern can drive parents to control and direct their children's actions, choices, and even friendships, in an effort to maintain a certain image in society.

For example, parents may discourage their children from pursuing hobbies or interests that are not considered "respectable" or "practical," instead steering them toward more traditional and socially accepted paths, such as medicine, engineering, or law. Similarly, parents may intervene in their children's social lives, choosing their friends or discouraging relationships that they believe could harm the family's reputation.

This focus on maintaining social standing can lead to a parenting style that prioritizes conformity and obedience over individuality and self-expression. While parents may believe they are acting in their child's best interests, this approach can stifle the child's ability to explore their own identity and make independent choices.

The Role of Gender Expectations: Gender expectations also play a significant role in shaping parenting behaviours in India. In many families, boys and girls are raised with different expectations and responsibilities, which can influence the degree of parental involvement in their lives. For example, girls may be expected to focus on domestic responsibilities and maintain a certain level of modesty, while boys may be encouraged to excel academically and pursue *careers that will ensure financial stability for the family.*

These gender-based expectations can lead to different forms of helicopter parenting, where parents may be more controlling of their daughters' social interactions and personal choices, while being more focused on their sons' academic achievements and career prospects. This can create a situation where children are not given the freedom to explore their own interests and develop their own identities, but are instead moulded to fit societal expectations.

The Psychological Impact of Helicopter Parenting

The psychological impact of helicopter parenting on children is a critical aspect to consider. While parents may have the best intentions, this style of parenting can have unintended consequences that affect a child's emotional and psychological well-being.

The Development of Anxiety and Stress: *One of the most significant psychological effects of helicopter parenting is the development of anxiety and stress in children. When parents are constantly involved in every aspect of their child's life, it can create a sense of pressure and expectation that the child may find overwhelming. The child may feel that they must always meet their parents' high standards and avoid making mistakes, leading to a fear of failure.*

This constant pressure can manifest as anxiety, where the child becomes excessively worried about their performance in school, their relationships with peers, and their ability to meet their parents' expectations. Over time, this anxiety can lead to more serious mental health issues, such as chronic stress, depression, and even burnout.

The Impact on Self-Esteem: *Helicopter parenting can also negatively impact a child's self-esteem. When parents are overly involved in their child's life, the child may begin to feel that they are not capable of making decisions or handling challenges on their own. This can lead to a lack of confidence in their own abilities and a reliance on their parents for guidance and approval.*

Children raised in a helicopter parenting environment may struggle to develop a strong sense of self-worth, as they are constantly seeking validation from their parents. This can make it difficult for them to develop a healthy self-image and can lead to feelings of inadequacy and low self-esteem.

The Lack of Independence and Resilience: *One of the most significant long-term effects of helicopter parenting is the lack of independence and resilience in children. When parents are constantly making decisions for their child and solving their problems, the child does not have the opportunity to develop the skills needed to navigate life's challenges on their own.*

As a result, children raised in a helicopter parenting environment may struggle with independence and decision-making in adulthood. They may become overly dependent on their parents or other authority figures and may lack the resilience needed to cope with setbacks and failures.

This lack of independence can also affect a child's ability to form healthy relationships. Without the opportunity to develop their own identity and make their own choices, they may struggle to establish boundaries and assert themselves in relationships with peers, colleagues, and even romantic partners.

The Impact of Technology on Helicopter Parenting

Technology has played a significant role in the rise of helicopter parenting, particularly in the context of modern life. Advances in technology have made it easier than ever for parents to monitor and control their children's activities, both online and offline.

Digital Surveillance and Parental Control: *With the advent of smartphones, GPS tracking apps, and social media, parents now have the ability to monitor their children's whereabouts, communications, and online activities in real-time. While these tools can be useful for ensuring a child's safety, they can also lead to an overreliance on digital surveillance, where parents feel the need to constantly check on their child's activities and whereabouts.*

This level of monitoring can create a sense of mistrust between parents and children, where the child feels that they are not trusted to make their own decisions or navigate the world on their own. It can also lead to a lack of privacy for the child, which can impact their ability to develop a healthy sense of autonomy.

The Influence of Social Media: *Social media has also contributed to the rise of helicopter parenting by* *creating a platform for parents to share and compare their children's achievements and milestones. While this can be a source of pride for parents, it can also create pressure to constantly showcase their child's success, leading to a more competitive and controlling approach to parenting.*

Parents may feel the need to curate their child's online presence, managing their social media profiles and controlling the content they post. This can limit the child's ability to express themselves freely and explore their own identity online.

Additionally, the constant exposure to curated images of other families' lives on social media can create unrealistic expectations for both parents and children. Parents may feel pressure to ensure their child is always performing well and achieving milestones, leading to increased involvement in their child's life.

Case Studies and Real-Life Examples

To better understand the impact of helicopter parenting, it is helpful to look at real-life examples and case studies that illustrate the challenges and consequences of this parenting style.

Academic Pressure and Burnout: *Consider the case of Aarti, a 16-year-old girl from a middle-class family in Mumbai. Aarti's parents have always placed a strong emphasis on academic success, enrolling her in multiple coaching classes and extracurricular activities from a young age. They closely monitor her grades and regularly check in with her teachers to ensure she is on track to excel in her board exams.*

While Aarti has always been a top-performing student, the pressure to maintain her academic success has taken a toll on her mental health. She often feels overwhelmed by her packed schedule and struggles with anxiety about meeting her parents' high expectations. Despite her achievements, Aarti feels a constant fear of failure and worries that she will disappoint her parents if she does not perform well.

This case illustrates how the intense pressure to succeed academically, combined with constant parental involvement, can lead to stress, anxiety, and burnout in children. While Aarti's parents are well-intentioned, their helicopter parenting approach has created a high-pressure environment that has negatively impacted her emotional well-being.

Lack of Independence and Decision-Making Skills: *Another example is Rohan, a 20-year-old college student from Delhi. Throughout his childhood, Rohan's parents were heavily involved in every aspect of his life, from choosing his hobbies to managing his friendships. They made most of his decisions for him, believing that they were protecting him from making mistakes.*

As a result, Rohan struggled with independence and decision-making when he moved away to college. He found it difficult to make decisions on his own, often seeking his parents' approval for even minor choices. This lack of independence made it challenging for him to navigate the challenges of college life, such as managing his time, making friends, and handling academic stress.

Rohan's experience highlights the long-term impact of helicopter parenting on a child's ability to develop independence and self-confidence. While his parents' intentions were to protect him, their over-involvement hindered his ability to develop the skills needed to navigate adulthood.

Finding Balance: Moving Towards Healthier Parenting

As we have seen, helicopter parenting, while rooted in love and concern, can have significant consequences for both parents and children. It is essential for parents to become more aware of the impact of their parenting style and to strive for a more balanced approach that supports their children's growth and development.

Encouraging Independence: *One of the key steps in moving away from helicopter parenting is encouraging independence in children. This involves giving children the space to make their own decisions, take on responsibilities, and learn from their mistakes. Parents can start by gradually giving their children more autonomy in areas such as schoolwork, hobbies, and social interactions.*

For example, instead of micromanaging a child's homework, parents can encourage them to set their own study schedule and manage their own assignments. If the child makes a mistake or misses a deadline, it can be used as a learning opportunity rather than a reason for punishment or criticism.

Encouraging independence also involves allowing children to take on age-appropriate responsibilities, such as managing their own pocket money, helping with household chores, or planning their own activities. These experiences help children develop essential life skills, such as problem-solving, time management, and decision-making.

Fostering Emotional Resilience: *Another important aspect of balanced parenting is fostering emotional resilience in children. Emotional resilience refers to the ability to cope with stress, setbacks, and challenges in a healthy and constructive way. It is an essential skill for navigating life's ups and downs and is often developed through experiences of overcoming difficulties.*

Parents can help foster emotional resilience by allowing their children to face challenges and solve problems on their own. This may involve stepping back and resisting the urge to immediately intervene when a child faces a difficult situation. Instead, parents can offer support and guidance while encouraging the child to come up with their own solutions.

It's also important for parents to model resilience themselves by demonstrating how they cope with stress and setbacks in their own lives. Children learn a great deal from observing their parents, and seeing how their parents handle challenges can help them develop their own coping strategies.

Building a Trusting Relationship: *Building a trusting relationship between parents and children is crucial for moving away from helicopter parenting. Trust involves believing in the child's ability to make good decisions and navigate the world on their own. It also involves open and honest communication, where the child feels* *comfortable sharing their thoughts, feelings, and experiences with their parents.*

To build trust, parents can start by listening to their child's perspective and respecting their opinions, even if they differ from their own. This involves allowing the child to express themselves without fear of judgment or punishment. By creating a safe and supportive environment, parents can help their children feel more confident in their abilities and more willing to take on challenges.

Trust also involves setting clear expectations and boundaries while giving the child the freedom to explore within those limits. For example, parents can set guidelines for curfew, screen time, and other activities, while allowing the child to make their own choices within those guidelines. This approach helps children develop a sense of responsibility and accountability while still feeling supported by their parents.

The Importance of Balance in Parenting

Helicopter parenting, while often well-intentioned, can have significant implications for both parents and children. It can lead to stress, anxiety, and a lack of independence in children, and can strain the parent-child relationship. As we move forward, it is essential for parents to become more aware of the impact of their parenting style and to strive for a balanced approach that supports their children's growth and development.

In the following chapters, we will explore the psychological aspects of helicopter parenting, its effects on children and families, and strategies for parents to adopt a healthier, more balanced approach to raising their children. Understanding the origins and motivations behind helicopter parenting is the first step toward making informed and positive changes in the way we nurture the next generation. By finding a balance between involvement and independence, parents can help their children develop the skills, confidence, and resilience they need to thrive in today's world

2. The Psychology Behind Helicopter Parenting

Why Do Parents Hover?

Parenting is one of the most challenging and rewarding experiences in life. Every parent wants the best for their child, aiming to protect them from harm, guide them toward success, and ensure their happiness. However, in this journey, some parents become overly involved in their children's lives, a behaviour known as helicopter parenting. But what drives this need to hover over every aspect of their child's life? Why do some parents find it difficult to let go and allow their children to grow independently?

In this chapter, we will explore the psychological factors that contribute to helicopter parenting. We will delve into the fears, anxieties, and motivations that lead parents to adopt this parenting style, and how their own need for control and perfection influences their behaviour. Understanding these underlying psychological aspects will help parents recognize these tendencies in themselves and consider healthier alternatives.

Parenting Motivations: Understanding the Fears and Anxieties

One of the primary reasons parents engage in helicopter parenting is the deep-seated fear of failure—both their child's failure and their own failure as parents. In today's competitive world, where success is often measured by academic achievements, career status, and social standing, parents feel an immense pressure to ensure their children excel in every aspect of life. This pressure can lead to anxiety about the future, prompting parents to take an overly controlling approach to their child's upbringing.

In India, where societal expectations and family honour often play a significant role, the pressure to succeed is even more pronounced. Parents may worry that if their child does not perform well academically, secure a prestigious job, or maintain a certain social image, it will reflect poorly on the family. These fears are further fuelled by comparisons with other families, where parents see other children achieving high marks, getting into top colleges, or landing lucrative jobs.

For example, imagine a parent who constantly hears about their neighbour's child excelling in school or winning awards. This parent might start to worry that their own child is not doing enough, leading them to push harder and become more involved in every aspect of their child's life. They might sign their child up for extra tuition classes, monitor their study habits closely, and intervene in their social life to ensure they are associating with the "right" peers. While these actions are motivated by love and concern, they can also stem from a fear of not measuring up to societal expectations.

Another common fear among helicopter parents is the fear of danger and harm. The world can be a scary place, and parents naturally want to protect their children from any potential risks. This protective instinct is a fundamental part of parenting, but when it becomes excessive, it can lead to helicopter parenting.

Parents who are constantly worried about their child's safety may become overly controlling, restricting their child's freedom to explore, take risks, and learn from their experiences.

For instance, a parent who is overly concerned about their child's safety might prevent them from participating in activities that other children their age enjoy, such as playing sports, going on school trips, or spending time with friends outside of school. While these restrictions are meant to protect the child, they can also limit the child's opportunities to develop independence and resilience.

The Need for Control: How Parents' Desire for Control Influences Their Behaviour

Another significant factor contributing to helicopter parenting is the parent's need for control. Some parents may have a strong desire to control every aspect of their child's life, from their academic performance to their social interactions and even their future career choices. This need for control can be driven by a variety of psychological factors, including the parent's own experiences, insecurities, and desire for perfection.

In many cases, the need for control stems from the parent's own upbringing. Parents who grew up in environments where they had little control over their own lives may try to compensate by exerting control over their children. For example, a parent who was raised in a strict household with rigid rules may have felt powerless as a child. As a parent, they might overcompensate by trying to control every detail of their child's life, believing that this will protect their child from the hardships they experienced.

Conversely, parents who were raised in chaotic or unstable environments may also develop a need for control. If a parent grew up in a household where there was a lack of structure or consistency, they might feel the need to create a highly controlled environment for their own children. This need for control can manifest in various ways, such as setting strict schedules, closely monitoring their child's activities, and making decisions on their child's behalf.

In Indian culture, where respect for authority and adherence to family traditions is highly valued, the need for control can be particularly strong. Parents may feel a sense of responsibility to ensure that their children follow a certain path, such as pursuing a specific career, marrying within the community, or maintaining the family's social status. This desire to uphold family values and traditions can lead parents to become overly involved in their child's decisions, from choosing their subjects in school to deciding on their life partners.

The Perfectionism Trap: When Good Intentions Go Too Far

Perfectionism is another psychological factor that can contribute to helicopter parenting. Parents who have high expectations for themselves and their children may fall into the trap of believing that anything less than perfection is unacceptable. This belief can lead to an intense focus on their child's achievements, behaviour, and overall performance, with little tolerance for mistakes or failures.

In the context of Indian society, where academic success is often seen as the key to a bright future, the pressure to achieve perfection can be overwhelming. Parents may push their children to excel in school, participate in multiple extracurricular activities, and achieve high marks, believing that this will secure their child's future success. However, this focus on perfection can have negative consequences, leading to stress, anxiety, and burnout for both the parent and the child.

Perfectionism can also manifest in other areas of life, such as social interactions and personal behaviour. For example, a parent who is focused on maintaining a perfect family image might become overly concerned with their child's behaviour in public, their choice of friends, or even their appearance. This can lead to a controlling and restrictive environment where the child feels they must always be on their best behaviour and meet high expectations, which can hinder their ability to develop a strong sense of self and independence.

Societal and Cultural Influences: The Role of Indian Culture in Helicopter Parenting

Societal and cultural factors play a significant role in shaping parenting styles, and this is particularly true in India. Indian culture places a strong emphasis on family, community, and social standing, which can influence parents' behaviour and attitudes toward raising their children. In many Indian families, there is a deep sense of duty and responsibility to ensure that children succeed and bring honour to the family.

This cultural emphasis on family honour and social status can contribute to helicopter parenting in several ways. Parents may feel a strong need to control their child's behaviour and decisions to ensure they align with cultural expectations and family values. For example, parents might be particularly concerned about their child's academic performance, choice of career, and social interactions, as these are often seen as reflections of the family's reputation.

In addition, the collectivist nature of Indian society, where the needs of the family and community are often prioritized over individual desires, can also contribute to helicopter parenting. Parents may feel that they need to make decisions on behalf of their children to ensure that they fulfil their familial and societal obligations. This can lead to a parenting style that is more directive and controlling, with less emphasis on the child's independence and autonomy.

The Influence of Social Media and Modern Technology

In today's digital age, social media and technology have added a new dimension to helicopter parenting. The rise of social media platforms has created a culture of constant comparison, where parents can easily compare their child's achievements and milestones with those of others. This can lead to increased pressure on parents to ensure their child is always performing well and meeting societal expectations.

For example, parents might feel the need to showcase their child's accomplishments on social media, such as high exam scores, awards, or participation in prestigious events. This can create a cycle of comparison and competition, where parents feel compelled to be more involved in their child's life to ensure they are keeping up with others. The constant exposure to curated images of other families' lives can also lead to unrealistic expectations, where parents feel they must always present a perfect image to the outside world.

Technology has also made it easier for parents to monitor and control their child's activities. With the advent of smartphones, GPS tracking apps, and social media, parents can now keep a close watch on their child's whereabouts, communications, and online activities. While these tools can provide a sense of security, they can also contribute to an overreliance on digital surveillance, where parents feel the need to constantly check on their child's activities and whereabouts.

Recognizing and Overcoming Helicopter Parenting Tendencies

Understanding the psychology behind helicopter parenting is the first step toward making positive changes in your parenting approach. By recognizing the fears, anxieties, and motivations that drive helicopter parenting, you can begin to challenge these tendencies and consider healthier alternatives that promote your child's independence and emotional well-being.

One way to start is by reflecting on your own upbringing and experiences. Consider how your own childhood experiences may have influenced your parenting style and whether you might be overcompensating for past challenges or insecurities. For example, if you grew up in a strict or chaotic environment, you might ask yourself whether your need for control is rooted in your own desire for stability or a fear of repeating past mistakes.

It's also important to examine your expectations for your child and consider whether they are realistic and appropriate for their age and developmental stage. While it's natural to want the best for your child, it's important to remember that mistakes and failures are a natural part of life and provide valuable opportunities for learning and growth. Allowing your child to experience these challenges and develop their own problem-solving skills is essential for their long-term success and independence.

Finally, consider how societal and cultural influences may be shaping your parenting approach. While it's important to honour family values and traditions, it's also essential to recognize the importance of fostering your child's individuality and autonomy. Striking a balance between maintaining cultural values and encouraging independence can help you create a healthy and supportive environment for your child's growth and development.

Striving for a Balanced Approach to Parenting

Helicopter parenting is often driven by a combination of love, fear, and a desire for control.

While these motivations are understandable, it's important to recognize the potential negative effects of this parenting style on your child's psychological well-being and development. By understanding the psychological factors that contribute to helicopter parenting, you can begin to make positive changes in your approach, fostering a more balanced and supportive environment for your child.

As parents, it's essential to remember that our role is to guide and support our children, not to control every aspect of their lives. By allowing them the freedom to explore, make mistakes, and learn from their experiences, we can help them develop the confidence, resilience, and independence they need to thrive in the world.

3. Children under the Lens: Consequences of Helicopter Parenting

The Ripple Effect of Over-Involvement

Helicopter parenting, while often well-intentioned, doesn't only affect the immediate family; its impact ripples out into the broader social world of both the parent and the child. The over-involvement of parents in every aspect of their child's life can lead to various social consequences, from the child's interactions with peers and authority figures to the parent's relationships with other adults. This chapter will explore how helicopter parenting affects the social development of children and the social dynamics within families and communities. Understanding these consequences is essential for parents who aim to foster not just their child's academic and personal growth but also their social and interpersonal skills.

The Impact on Peer Relationships

One of the most significant areas where helicopter parenting exerts its influence is in the child's ability to form and maintain peer relationships. Social skills are critical for a child's overall development, as they help build friendships, navigate social situations, and develop empathy. However, when parents are overly involved in their child's social interactions, it can hinder the development of these essential skills.

Children learn to interact with others through experience—by making friends, resolving conflicts, and understanding social cues. When parents constantly step in to manage their child's social life, they deprive the child of these learning opportunities. For instance, a parent who always chooses their child's friends, mediates disputes, or organizes social activities may prevent the child from learning how to do these things independently.

In Indian society, where family and community play a central role, social interactions are often closely monitored by parents. This can be particularly true in cases where parents are concerned about their child's associations and the potential influence of peers. While this concern is understandable, it's important for children to have the freedom to choose their friends and navigate social dynamics on their own. Over time, children who are not given this freedom may struggle with social independence, finding it difficult to establish and maintain friendships without parental involvement.

Moreover, children of helicopter parents may develop a dependency on their parents in social situations. They might look to their parents for guidance or approval before making decisions, even in simple social scenarios, such as choosing who to sit with during lunch or how to approach a group of peers. This can lead to a lack of confidence in social settings, making it harder for the child to form meaningful connections with others.

Authority and Social Boundaries

Another critical aspect of social development affected by helicopter parenting is the child's relationship with authority figures, such as teachers, coaches, and even extended family members. When parents are overly involved in their child's interactions with authority figures, it can blur the lines of respect and boundaries, making it difficult for the child to navigate these relationships appropriately.

In many cases, helicopter parents might intervene on behalf of their child in situations involving authority figures, such as questioning a teacher's grading, challenging a coach's decisions, or stepping in during disagreements with extended family members. While these actions are often motivated by a desire to protect the child, they can undermine the authority of the adults involved and send the message that the child does not need to respect or follow their guidance.

In the Indian context, where respect for elders and authority figures are deeply ingrained in cultural norms, this can create confusion for the child. On the one hand, they are taught to respect authority, but on the other hand, they see their parents challenging these figures on their behalf. This can lead to mixed messages about how to interact with authority figures and where the boundaries of respect lie.

Furthermore, children who are used to having their parents intervene in these situations may struggle with authority in other settings, such as school or later in the workplace. They might expect the same level of intervention and support in these environments, leading to difficulties in accepting feedback, criticism, or direction from others. This can hinder their ability to function effectively in structured environments where respect for authority and adherence to rules are essential.

Family Dynamics and Relationships

Helicopter parenting doesn't only affect the child; it also has a profound impact on family dynamics and relationships. The constant involvement of parents in their child's life can create tension and strain within the family, as well as affect the parent's relationship with other family members, including their spouse, other children, and extended family.

For instance, in a family where one child is the focus of helicopter parenting, other siblings may feel neglected or resentful. They might perceive that their needs and desires are being overlooked in favour of the child who receives the most attention. This can lead to sibling rivalry, resentment, and a sense of inequality within the family. Over time, these feelings can erode the bond between siblings and create long-lasting rifts in the family.

In addition, the relationship between parents can also be affected by helicopter parenting. When one parent is overly focused on the child, it can create an imbalance in the parental partnership, where the other parent may feel excluded or undervalued. This can lead to disagreements and conflicts, particularly if the other parent has a different approach to parenting or feels that their role in the child's life is being diminished.

Extended family members, such as grandparents, aunts, and uncles, may also feel the effects of helicopter parenting. In many Indian families, extended family members play an important role in a child's upbringing, offering guidance, support, and wisdom. However, helicopter parents might limit or control these interactions, believing that they know what's best for their child. This can create tension and conflict within the larger family network, as well as deprive the child of valuable relationships with other family members.

The Parent's Social Life and Well-Being

Helicopter parenting can also take a toll on the parent's own social life and well-being. When parents devote all their time and energy to managing their child's life, they may neglect their own needs and relationships. This can lead to social isolation, burnout, and a sense of identity loss, as the parent's life becomes entirely cantered around their child.

In Indian culture, where community and social connections are highly valued, this isolation can be particularly challenging. Parents who are overly focused on their child may find themselves withdrawing from social activities, community events, and even relationships with friends and family. Over time, this can lead to feelings of loneliness and dissatisfaction, as the parent's social world becomes increasingly narrow.

Moreover, the stress of constantly managing their child's life can lead to burnout, where the parent feels exhausted, overwhelmed, and emotionally drained. This can have serious consequences for the parent's mental and physical health, as well as their ability to effectively parent their child. In extreme cases, this burnout can lead to resentment towards the child or a sense of failure as a parent, further complicating the family dynamic.

The Child's Transition to Adulthood

One of the most significant social consequences of helicopter parenting is its impact on the child's transition to adulthood. As children grow up, they need to develop the skills and confidence to navigate the adult world independently. However, helicopter parenting can hinder this process, leaving the child unprepared for the challenges of adulthood.

Children who have been raised with helicopter parenting may struggle with key aspects of adult life, such as making decisions, managing responsibilities, and forming independent relationships. They might feel anxious or uncertain about stepping out into the world on their own, as they are used to having their parents' guide and support them in every aspect of their lives.

For example, a young adult who has always had their parents manage their schedule, handle their conflicts, or make decisions for them may find it difficult to navigate the demands of college or the workplace. They might struggle with time management, conflict resolution, or decision-making, leading to feelings of inadequacy or failure. This can create a cycle of dependency, where the young adult continues to rely on their parents for support and guidance, even when they should be developing their own independence.

In Indian society, where the transition to adulthood often involves significant milestones, such as pursuing higher education, entering the workforce, or getting married, the effects of helicopter parenting can be particularly pronounced. Young adults who are unprepared for these transitions may struggle to meet the expectations of their family and society, leading to stress, anxiety, and a sense of failure.

Breaking the Cycle: Promoting Healthy Social Development

Understanding the social consequences of helicopter parenting is the first step towards making positive changes in your parenting approach. By recognizing the impact of over-involvement on your child's social development, you can begin to foster healthier, more independent relationships for both yourself and your child.

One of the most important steps you can take is to gradually step back and allow your child to take more control over their social interactions and decisions. This doesn't mean abandoning your role as a parent, but rather shifting from a directive to a supportive role. Encourage your child to make their own decisions, resolve conflicts independently, and navigate social situations on their own. Offer guidance and support when needed, but resist the urge to take over or intervene unless absolutely necessary.

It's also important to model healthy social behaviour for your child. Show them how to build and maintain positive relationships, set boundaries, and handle conflicts in a respectful and constructive manner. By demonstrating these skills in your own relationships, you can provide your child with a strong foundation for their social development.

In addition, take time to nurture your own social life and well-being. Make time for your own friendships, hobbies, and interests, and don't be afraid to ask for help or support when needed. By maintaining a balanced life, you can prevent burnout and ensure that you have the energy and emotional resilience to be the best parent you can be.

Conclusion: Striving for Balance in Social Development

Helicopter parenting can have far-reaching social consequences, affecting not only the child's ability to form and maintain relationships but also the parent's own social life and well-being. By understanding these consequences and taking steps to promote healthy social development, you can help your child develop the confidence.

4. The Toll on Parents

Helicopter parenting is a double-edged sword; while parents often engage in this style of parenting with the best intentions, the toll it takes on them can be significant. This chapter delves into the multifaceted impact of helicopter parenting on parents, focusing on the emotional, psychological, and relational consequences. We will explore how the constant vigilance and over-involvement in their children's lives can lead to parental burnout, strained marital relationships, and conflicts within the family. Through real-life examples relevant to Indian readers, we'll see how these challenges manifest and what can be done to alleviate them.

Parental Burnout: The Hidden Cost of Over-Involvement

Understanding Parental Burnout: *Parental burnout is a state of chronic exhaustion that can occur when parents are overly involved in their children's lives. Unlike the more commonly discussed burnout in professional settings, parental burnout is specifically linked to the intense demands of parenting. Helicopter parents, who micromanage every aspect of their child's life, are particularly susceptible to this condition.*

Parental burnout often manifests as physical exhaustion, emotional detachment from the child, and a sense of ineffectiveness in the parental role. Over time, these feelings can lead to more severe consequences, such as depression or anxiety. The societal pressures to be a "perfect parent," especially in a competitive environment like India, only exacerbate these feelings.

The Case of Mrs. Verma from Delhi *Mrs. Verma is a quintessential example of a helicopter parent in an urban Indian setting. Living in a bustling neighbourhood of Delhi, Mrs. Verma's day begins before sunrise. She meticulously prepares breakfast for her two teenagers, ensuring each meal is balanced with the right nutrients. She supervises their morning routine, making sure they leave for school on time with everything they might need, from completed homework to the right sports gear.*

Throughout the school day, Mrs. Verma is constantly on edge, checking the tracking app on her phone to monitor her children's whereabouts. She worries if her daughter misses a class or if her son doesn't finish his lunch. The evenings are no different, as she spends hours helping them with homework, even going so far as to redo assignments to ensure they receive the highest grades possible.

Initially, Mrs. Verma felt a sense of pride and accomplishment in her dedication. But over time, the relentless pressure began to take its toll. She started experiencing chronic fatigue, sleepless nights, and frequent headaches. Her patience wore thin, leading to irritability and frustration. Simple tasks became overwhelming, and she found herself emotionally drained. The joy of parenting was replaced by a sense of duty and exhaustion.

Mrs. Verma's experience is not unique. In cities across India, many parents find themselves caught in a similar cycle. The desire to provide the best for their children, fuelled by societal expectations and competitive academic environments, often leads to burnout. This scenario underscores the importance of recognizing the signs of parental burnout early and taking proactive steps to address it.

The Cultural Pressure to Excel: *In India, the pressure to excel academically is immense. Parents often feel a deep responsibility to ensure their children succeed, not just for their own satisfaction but also to meet societal expectations. This cultural pressure can amplify the tendencies of helicopter parents, pushing them to become even more involved in their children's lives.*

For instance, the education system in India is highly competitive, with intense pressure to secure admission into prestigious schools and colleges. This has led to a culture where parents feel compelled to manage every aspect of their child's education, from choosing the right school to overseeing their study schedule and extracurricular activities. In such an environment, the risk of parental burnout increases significantly.

The Overwhelming Life of Mr. and Mrs. Singh from Mumbai *Mr. and Mrs. Singh, living in a high-rise apartment in Mumbai, were determined to provide their daughter with the best education possible. They enrolled her in a renowned international school, participated in every parent-teacher meeting, and ensured she had access to all possible resources. They even hired private tutors for subjects they felt she needed extra help with.*

Their lives revolved around their daughter's academic success. Mrs. Singh would spend hours researching educational methods and curriculums, while Mr. Singh would handle the financial aspects, working overtime to afford the high tuition fees and additional expenses. They had little time for themselves, their social lives dwindled, and their conversations increasingly cantered around their daughter's progress.

Despite their efforts, the Singhs began to feel the strain. Mrs. Singh developed anxiety, constantly worrying about her daughter's performance, while Mr. Singh became irritable and distant, consumed by work-related stress. The relentless focus on their daughter's success left them both physically and emotionally exhausted.

Relationship Strains: The Ripple Effect of Helicopter Parenting

Impact on Marital Relationships: *One of the most significant but often overlooked consequences of helicopter parenting is the strain it can place on the marital relationship. When parents are overly focused on their children, they often neglect their own relationship, leading to misunderstandings, resentment, and emotional distance.*

In many cases, the division of parenting responsibilities can become uneven, with one parent taking on the bulk of the work, either out of a sense of duty or because they believe they can do it better. This can create feelings of imbalance and unfairness in the relationship, leading to conflicts and, in some cases, even separation.

The Misunderstandings of Mr. and Mrs. Iyer from Bangalore *Mr. and Mrs. Iyer were a couple who enjoyed a close, loving relationship. However, things changed when their son entered high school. Mrs. Iyer, an involved and caring mother, became increasingly focused on their son's academic performance. She took it upon herself to attend every parent-teacher meeting, supervise his study schedule, and manage his extracurricular activities, believing that her involvement was crucial to his success.*

Mr. Iyer, on the other hand, believed that their son needed more independence and that it was important for him to learn to manage his own time and responsibilities. He was supportive of his wife but felt that she was overdoing it. Over time, this difference in parenting styles led to frequent disagreements. Mrs. Iyer felt that her husband was not supportive enough and accused him of being indifferent to their son's future, while Mr. Iyer felt sidelined and unappreciated, leading to a growing sense of disconnect between them.

The once-strong bond between Mr. and Mrs. Iyer began to weaken, and they found themselves arguing more often, not just about their son but about other aspects of their lives as well. The stress of helicopter parenting had spilled over into their marriage, creating a rift that neither had anticipated.

This example illustrates how helicopter parenting can strain even the strongest relationships. The focus on the child's needs, while well-intentioned, can lead to a neglect of the marital relationship, causing emotional distance and resentment. It highlights the importance of maintaining a balance between parenting responsibilities and nurturing the marital bond.

Family Dynamics: The Clash of Generations *In many Indian households, especially in joint families, grandparents play a significant role in raising children. Their involvement can be a source of support for parents, providing additional care and guidance. However, when parents adopt a helicopter parenting style, it can lead to conflicts with grandparents who may have a more relaxed approach to parenting.*

The clash of parenting styles can create tension within the family, as parents may feel that their methods are being undermined, while grandparents may feel excluded or unappreciated. This can disrupt the harmony of the household and create stress for all involved.

The Rao Family Conflict in Hyderabad *In the Rao family, who lived in a joint family setup in Hyderabad, the grandparents had always been involved in the upbringing of their grandchildren. They believed in giving the children the freedom to play, explore, and learn from their own experiences. However, their daughter-in-law, Mrs. Rao, had a different approach. She was a helicopter parent who believed in closely monitoring every aspect of her children's lives.*

Mrs. Rao would often clash with her in-laws over how to handle the children. She wanted to control their daily routines, decide their extracurricular activities, and even dictate their diet, while the grandparents felt that she was being overly restrictive and stifling the children's natural growth. The tension between Mrs. Rao and her in-laws grew, leading to frequent arguments and a strained atmosphere in the household.

This situation is not uncommon in Indian joint families, where differing parenting styles can lead to discord. The Rao family's experience highlights the importance of finding a middle ground where both parents and grandparents can contribute to the child's upbringing in a way that respects each other's perspectives.

Strategies for Parents to Avoid Burnout and Relationship Strain

To mitigate the effects of helicopter parenting on themselves and their relationships, parents need to adopt strategies that promote balance and well-being. Here are some practical steps:

1. **Prioritize Self-Care:**

    Parents need to recognize that they cannot pour from an empty cup. Taking time for themselves is crucial for maintaining their well-being and preventing burnout. Engaging in activities they enjoy, whether it's a hobby, exercise, or simply relaxing, can help recharge their energy and improve their mood.

For example, Mrs. Verma could benefit from setting aside time each day for activities like yoga or reading, which would allow her to decompress and regain her sense of self.

2. Open Communication:

Couples should have open and honest discussions about their parenting approaches. It's essential to find a middle ground that respects both parents' perspectives and allows them to work as a team. Regular communication can help prevent misunderstandings and ensure that both partners feel supported.

Mr. and Mrs. Iyer could establish regular "couple time" where they can reconnect and discuss their concerns without the distractions of daily life. This would help them strengthen their relationship and align their parenting strategies.

3. Involve the Extended Family:

Embracing the support of extended family members, such as grandparents, can be beneficial. Their experience and wisdom can provide valuable insights, and their involvement can ease the pressure on parents. It's important to set clear boundaries and expectations so that everyone feels valued and respected.

In the Rao family, setting boundaries that allow both parents and grandparents to contribute to the child's upbringing could create a more harmonious household, where different perspectives are respected and integrated.

4. **Delegate Responsibilities:**

    Parents should not hesitate to delegate tasks to their children and encourage them to take responsibility for their own lives. This not only reduces the burden on parents but also helps children develop independence and self-confidence.

    For instance, Mr. and Mrs. Singh could gradually encourage their daughter to manage her study schedule and take ownership of her responsibilities, which would reduce their stress and help their daughter develop important life skills.

5. **Seek Professional Help:**

    If burnout or relationship strain becomes overwhelming, seeking the guidance of a counsellor or therapist can provide valuable insights and coping strategies. Professional help can assist parents in navigating the challenges of helicopter parenting and finding healthier ways to support their children.

6. **Setting Realistic Expectations:**

Parents often set high expectations for themselves, believing that they must be perfect in every aspect of parenting. However, it's important to recognize that perfection is unattainable, and it's okay to make mistakes. Setting realistic expectations can help reduce stress and prevent burnout.

For example, Mrs. Verma could benefit from acknowledging that it's okay to let her children face challenges on their own, rather than trying to solve every problem for them.

7. **Balancing Involvement with Independence:**

Finding the right balance between being involved in your child's life and giving them the independence to grow is crucial. Parents should aim to be supportive without being overbearing, allowing their children to learn from their experiences.

In the case of Mr. and Mrs. Iyer, encouraging their son to take responsibility for his own studies and extracurricular activities could foster independence while still providing guidance when needed.

Navigating the Challenges of Helicopter Parenting

Helicopter parenting, while often motivated by love and concern, can have unintended negative effects on parents, leading to burnout, strained relationships, and conflicts within the family. By recognizing these challenges and implementing strategies to mitigate them, parents can maintain their well-being while still being supportive and involved in their children's lives.

Balancing involvement with self-care, open communication, and the inclusion of extended family members is a key to avoiding the pitfalls of helicopter parenting. Ultimately, finding a middle ground where parents can be engaged without overwhelming themselves is essential for ensuring a happier, healthier family dynamic.

5. The Role of Technology

In today's fast-paced world, technology has become a central figure in our lives, especially in the realm of parenting. If you think about it, parenting in the digital age is like trying to cook a gourmet meal while riding a unicycle—juggling safety, privacy, and independence all at once. Technology offers a plethora of tools that can act as a safety net or an overbearing presence, and finding the right balance can be a challenge. This chapter will explore how technology has changed parenting, especially in the Indian context, and offer a humorous look at how these tools can sometimes create more chaos than calm.

Digital Surveillance: Parenting in the Age of Technology

The Rise of Digital Monitoring: *In the pre-digital era, parents relied on their intuition or the watchful eye of a neighbour to keep tabs on their children. Now, we have an arsenal of digital tools at our disposal: GPS tracking apps, parental control software, and even smart home devices that can monitor everything from the temperature of the house to the number of steps taken. While these tools are designed to enhance safety, they often lead to what we call "over-parenting," where parents become so involved that their children might as well be on a reality TV show.*

The Overzealous Sharma Family of Delhi *Consider the Sharma family from Delhi, where Mrs. Sharma has embraced technology with the enthusiasm of a kid in a candy store. She has installed a GPS app that tracks her son Aryan's every move. Aryan, who is 16 and just* *wants to hang out with friends, feels like he's under constant surveillance, One day, Aryan decided to take a detour to grab a samosa. Within minutes, his phone buzzed with a message from his mom: "Why did you just pass by the chaat stall on MG Road? Are you meeting that boy I don't like?" Aryan sighed, realizing that even his samosa cravings were under scrutiny. This situation is a familiar one in many Indian households, where technology intended for safety ends up making children feel trapped in a virtual cage.*

The Psychological Impact of Constant Monitoring: *Digital surveillance provides parents with peace of mind, but it can also create a sense of paranoia and overprotection. Instead of worrying if their child is eating well or dressing warmly, parents now obsess over every minute detail. Children may feel suffocated by the constant scrutiny, leading to a strained relationship. Imagine a teenager who's used to a degree of independence suddenly having every move scrutinized. It's a recipe for rebellion or, at the very least, some creative ways to sneak around.*

The Great Escape of Rohan from Pune *Rohan, a 16-year-old from Pune, was fed up with his parents' digital monitoring. His parents had installed an app that tracked not only his location but also his screen time and social media use. Every evening, Rohan faced an inquisition about his online activities. One weekend, Rohan handed his phone to a friend who was visiting the library and sneaked off to the movies. When his parents saw his phone's location at the library for hours, they were puzzled. Rohan's brief taste of freedom was quickly overshadowed by a long lecture* *about trust and responsibility, but it was worth it for him. Rohan's story illustrates how technology, when misused, can lead to a cat-and-mouse game between parents and their children.*

The New Frontier of Digital Parenting: *As technology advances, so too do the methods of digital parenting. New gadgets and apps are constantly being introduced, each promising to make parenting easier or more secure. However, these tools often come with their own set of challenges and can sometimes exacerbate the very issues they are meant to solve.*

The Parental Control App Drama of the Mehta Family
The Mehta family from Bangalore decided to try out the latest parental control app, which promised to filter inappropriate content and limit screen time. What started as a well-intentioned move quickly spiralled into chaos. The app was so stringent that it blocked access to not just games and social media but also educational websites. When their daughter, Ananya, was unable to access her online study materials, she was understandably frustrated. The app's overzealous nature led to family arguments and a realization that sometimes less is more when it comes to digital parenting.

Social Media and Parental Involvement

The Influence of Social Media on Parenting: *Social media has changed the way parents interact with their children's lives. While it provides a platform to share milestones and stay connected, it also creates a pressure cooker environment where parents feel the need to document every achievement and moment. In India,* *where social status and public perception can be of high importance, this pressure can be particularly intense. Parents might feel compelled to showcase their children as perfect little angels, leading to unnecessary stress for both the parent and the child.*

The Social Media Struggles of Mrs. Patel from Mumbai
Mrs. Patel from Mumbai is a social media maven. Her Instagram feed is a gallery of her daughter Riya's achievements—whether it's winning a school competition or making a decorative Rakhi. While Mrs. Patel's friends and followers admire her curated posts, Riya feels like she's on display 24/7. When her mom posted a photo of her winning a debate competition, complete with a detailed account and a childhood photo, Riya was mortified. The post garnered plenty of likes but left Riya feeling exposed and embarrassed. This scenario is a common pitfall of social media, where parents' best intentions to celebrate their children can sometimes backfire, causing frustration and a sense of betrayal.

The Quest for the Perfect Post: *Parents today often find themselves in a constant quest for the perfect social media post—one that showcases their children's accomplishments while garnering approval from their online community. This can lead to a cycle of competition, where parents feel pressured to outdo each other in the realm of social media parenting.*

The Instagram Influencer Mom, Mrs. Kapoor *Mrs. Kapoor, a proud mother from Chandigarh, turned her daughter's school achievements into an art form. From creating elaborate Instagram stories about every school* *event to hosting "proud mom" photo shoots, Mrs. Kapoor became a local celebrity among other parents. While her intentions were to celebrate her daughter's success, the constant focus on social media left her daughter feeling like a prize on display. The irony was not lost on Mrs. Kapoor when she realized that her quest for the perfect post had led to unintended consequences in her family life.*

The Impact on Parent-Child Relationships: *Oversharing on social media can strain the parent-child relationship, especially as children grow older and their desire for privacy increases. When parents share too much online without considering their child's feelings, it can lead to conflicts and feelings of betrayal. Teenagers, in particular, may find it challenging to navigate their online presence while dealing with their parents' social media enthusiasm.*

The Instagram Incident with Kavya from Chennai *Kavya, a 15-year-old from Chennai, had just won a major debate competition and was looking forward to celebrating with friends. But her excitement was dampened when her mother posted a lengthy, sentimental tribute on Instagram, including photos and a detailed story about her achievements. Kavya's friends saw the post, and she felt embarrassed and exposed. When she confronted her mother, it led to an argument where Kavya expressed her frustration about her life being broadcasted online. This incident highlights the need for parents to consider their child's perspective before sharing online, ensuring that their actions don't infringe on their child's privacy or autonomy.*

Balancing Safety and Independence

Finding the Line between Protection and Overreach: *One of the greatest challenges of modern parenting is balancing the use of technology to protect your child while allowing them the independence they need to thrive. It's tempting to use every tool at your disposal to ensure safety, but children also need space to grow, make mistakes, and learn from their experiences.*

Strategies for Balanced Digital Parenting:

Set Clear Boundaries:

Establish clear guidelines for using digital tools. For example, use tracking apps only for specific purposes, like long trips or unfamiliar places, and avoid monitoring every little detail. This helps maintain trust and reduces the feeling of being constantly watched. It's also essential to communicate these boundaries to your child, so they understand the rationale behind them.

Foster Open Communication:

Encourage regular conversations about online safety and responsible behaviour. Instead of relying on technology to monitor every move, build a relationship where your child feels comfortable discussing their online activities and any issues they encounter. This open line of communication can help prevent misunderstandings and foster a sense of trust.

Respect Privacy:

As children grow older, their need for privacy becomes more pronounced. Respect their space and avoid intrusive monitoring. Focus on building a trust-based relationship rather than relying solely on digital tools. Allowing children to have private conversations and personal spaces helps them develop independence and self-confidence.

Teach Digital Literacy:

Equip your children with the knowledge and skills to navigate the digital world responsibly. Teach them about online privacy, potential dangers, and how to use technology safely. Empowering them with this knowledge helps them make informed decisions and protects them from online risks.

Encourage Independence:

Gradually give your children more freedom as they demonstrate responsibility. Allow them to make their own decisions and learn from their experiences. This builds confidence and prepares them for the challenges of adulthood. Encourage them to take on responsibilities and make choices, even if it means making mistakes along the way.

The Gupta Family's Balanced Approach from Pune *The Gupta family from Pune has mastered the art of balancing technology and parenting. They use a GPS tracking app, but with clear boundaries—only checking it during long journeys or when the children are in unfamiliar places. They also have regular discussions* *about online safety, rather than relying on constant monitoring. This approach has fostered trust and independence in their children while providing a safety net when needed. Their balanced approach exemplifies how technology can be used effectively without becoming an overbearing presence.*

The Balanced Approach of the Patel Family from Ahmedabad *The Patel family from Ahmedabad is another great example of balanced digital parenting. Mr. Patel, a tech-savvy dad, has set up parental controls on his kids' devices but has made it a point to discuss with them why these controls are in place. He encourages his children to approach him with any concerns or questions about their online activities. This approach has led to a healthy balance where the children feel secure but also have the freedom to explore the digital world responsibly. Mr. Patel's method shows that technology, when used thoughtfully, can support parenting goals without undermining a child's autonomy.*

Navigating Technology in Parenting

Technology has revolutionized parenting, offering new tools and opportunities to keep children safe and connected. However, it has also introduced new challenges, particularly in the realm of helicopter parenting. The key to navigating these challenges is finding a balance between using technology for protection and allowing children the independence they need to grow and develop.

Parents must be mindful of the impact that digital surveillance and social media can have on their relationship with their children. By setting clear boundaries, fostering open communication, and respecting their child's privacy, parents can use technology in a way that enhances safety without compromising trust and autonomy.

In the end, while technology can be a valuable ally, it's no substitute for good old-fashioned parenting, complete with patience, understanding, and the occasional goofy dance party to lighten the mood. Balancing these elements will help you raise well-adjusted, independent children who are capable of navigating the complexities of the digital world with confidence and responsibility. So, put away the digital magnifying glass, have a laugh, and remember that parenting in the digital age is as much about connection and trust as it is about using the latest gadgets.

6. Case Studies and Real-Life Examples

Learning from Real-Life Experiences

Understanding the concept of helicopter parenting is one thing, but seeing how it plays out in real life can provide invaluable insights. In this chapter, we will explore a series of case studies and real-life examples that illustrate the effects of helicopter parenting on both parents and children. These stories come from a range of perspectives, including those of parents, children, and professionals such as psychologists, educators, and counsellors. By examining these accounts, we can gain a deeper understanding of the challenges and consequences of helicopter parenting, as well as the potential pathways to healthier parenting practices.

Stories from Parents and Children: First-Hand Accounts

Case Study 1

The Overprotective Parent and the Struggling Student

Neha, a mother of two, prided herself on being deeply involved in her children's lives. Her son, Arjun, was a bright student in primary school, but as he entered high school, Neha noticed that his grades began to slip. Concerned, she took it upon herself to manage every aspect of Arjun's academic life. She would review his homework, help him with projects, and even communicate with his teachers on his behalf to ensure he was on track.

At first, this approach seemed to work. Arjun's grades improved slightly, but over time, he began to show signs of stress and burnout. He became increasingly dependent on his mother to complete assignments and lacked confidence in his abilities. When it came time for exams, Arjun would panic, feeling overwhelmed by the pressure to perform.

Neha, realizing that her involvement might be contributing to his anxiety, decided to step back. She encouraged Arjun to take responsibility for his studies, offering support only when he asked for it. The transition was difficult for both of them, but gradually, Arjun began to regain his confidence. He learned to manage his time, study effectively, and seek help when needed. By the end of high school, Arjun was more independent and prepared for the challenges of college life.

This case highlights the fine line between being supportive and being overprotective. Neha's intentions were good, but her over-involvement initially hindered Arjun's ability to develop the skills he needed to succeed on his own.

Case Study 2

The Micromanaged Child and the Struggles of Adulthood

Ravi was a young adult who had grown up in a household where his parents micromanaged every aspect of his life. From his childhood, his parents made decisions for him—what he should wear, who he should be friends with, and even what career path he should follow. They believed they were guiding him toward success, but as Ravi entered adulthood, he found himself struggling to make decisions on his own.

After completing his engineering degree, a choice made by his parents, Ravi was offered a job in a different city. While his parents were excited about the opportunity, Ravi felt paralyzed by fear. He had never lived away from home or made significant decisions independently. The thought of moving to a new city, managing his finances, and starting a job without his parents' guidance filled him with anxiety.

Ravi's story illustrates the long-term consequences of helicopter parenting. His parents' desire to control his life left him ill-prepared for the challenges of adulthood. Recognizing this, Ravi sought help from a counselor who worked with him to develop decision-making skills and build confidence. Over time, Ravi learned to trust his instincts and take responsibility for his life. While the transition was challenging, it ultimately led to greater independence and personal growth.

Case Study 3

The Well-Meaning Parent and the Socially Isolated Child

Anita was a stay-at-home mother who devoted her time to ensuring her daughter, Riya, had the best possible upbringing. Anita organized playdates, supervised all of Riya's activities, and even decided which friends she could spend time with. Anita believed that by controlling Riya's social circle, she could protect her from bad influences and ensure she made the "right" friends.

As Riya grew older, she became increasingly isolated. She struggled to make friends on her own, relying on her mother to facilitate her social interactions. At school, Riya found it difficult to connect with her peers, often feeling out of place and unsure of how to initiate conversations or join group activities.

By the time she reached high school, Riya's social anxiety had become a significant issue. She felt lonely and disconnected, which affected her self-esteem and overall well-being. Anita, realizing the unintended consequences of her actions, sought advice from a child psychologist. The psychologist recommended gradually giving Riya more freedom to make her own social choices, encouraging her to join clubs and activities that interested her.

With time, Riya began to develop her social skills and form friendships on her own. While the journey was not easy, Riya eventually found a group of friends with whom she felt comfortable and accepted. This case underscores the importance of allowing children to navigate their social world independently, even if it means they make mistakes along the way.

Professional Perspectives: Insights from Psychologists, Educators, and Counsellors

Insight 1: The Psychological Impact of Over-Involvement

Dr. Meera Joshi, a clinical psychologist with over 20 years of experience, has seen the effects of helicopter parenting in her practice. She explains that children who grow up with overly involved parents often struggle with issues of self-esteem and autonomy. "These children may come to believe that they are incapable of handling life's challenges on their own," she says. "They've internalized the idea that their parents need to step in and solve their problems, which can lead to a lack of confidence and an inability to cope with stress."

Dr. Joshi emphasizes the importance of fostering independence from a young age. "Parents should gradually increase their child's responsibilities and allow them to make decisions, even if it means they might fail sometimes. Failure is a crucial part of learning and developing resilience."

She also notes that helicopter parenting can lead to anxiety and depression in children. "When children feel they are constantly being watched or judged by their parents, it can create immense pressure. This can result in anxiety, and in some cases, depression, as the child feels they can never meet the high expectations set for them."

Insight 2: The Educational Perspective

Mr. Rajiv Sinha, a veteran school principal in Delhi, has observed the rise of helicopter parenting over the past two decades. "We see more and more parents who are heavily involved in their child's education to the point where it becomes counterproductive," he says. "They often do their child's homework, intervene in every small issue, and put enormous pressure on the child to perform academically."

Mr. Sinha argues that this level of involvement can hinder a child's natural curiosity and love for learning. "When parents take over, children lose the opportunity to explore subjects on their own, to experiment, and to learn from their mistakes. This can lead to a lack of motivation and a dependency on external validation, rather than developing a genuine interest in learning."

He advises parents to trust their children and the educational process. "Teachers are trained to guide students through their learning journey. Parents should support their children, but they should also allow them to navigate their education independently. This will help children develop critical thinking skills and a sense of responsibility for their own learning."

Insight 3: The Counsellor's View on Family Dynamics

Mrs. Lakshmi Nair, a family counsellor based in Bangalore, has worked with many families dealing with the challenges of helicopter parenting. She points out that this parenting style can lead to significant strain within the family unit. "When one child receives all the attention, it can create resentment among siblings and tension between the parents. The family dynamic becomes unbalanced, which can lead to long-term emotional and relational issues."

Mrs. Nair encourages families to adopt a more balanced approach to parenting. "It's important for parents to recognize that their role is to guide and support, not to control. By focusing on open communication and mutual respect, families can create a healthier environment where every member feels valued and supported."

She also stresses the importance of setting boundaries, both for the child and for the parents. "Parents need to give their children space to grow and develop their own identities. At the same time, they need to maintain their own lives, interests, and relationships outside of their parenting role. This balance is the key to maintaining a healthy family dynamic."

Insight 4: Parenting Style as Endless Possibility to Child's Development

Vijander Singh, Ph.D.-Psychology adds that a continued debate persists from past five to six decades regarding role of parenting in the growth of child across cultures and continents. Majority of literature available support the western views regarding types of parenting styles viz. Authoritative, Permissive/Indulgent, Neglecting and Authoritarian. In authoritative punishment or negative reinforcement is usually infrequent, still authoritative parents are not too permissive or not too strict. They are thought to be supportive of Baumrind's "Just Right" notion. Permissive or Indulgent parenting is considered as no frill parenting where children get full freedom and autonomy. Neglectful parenting assumes indifference, lack of empathy and no emotional attachment. There is a complete absence of expectations or demands from the child. In Authoritarian parenting there are excessive demands from the child as if the child is responsible for parents' fate. Parents are hardly permissive but impose strict rules to be followed in the name of discipline. There is no scope of child personal choices.

There is no guideline or standard operating protocol for Parenting but still it is the most beautiful, yet complicated exercise. Every child is different genotypically and phenotypically and every parent learns special skills to shape their social, emotional, and cognitive development. It is an interactive effect of the factors such as culture, values, and behavioral experiences.

Of these the outcomes of authoritative parenting have been expressed in more academic achievement. Children use adaptive strategies frequently than to no-adaptive ones and lower levels of failure expectations. They primarily use self-enhancing attributions rather than blaming others. On the other hand, neglected families are responsible for child's maladaptive strategies and passivity, which in turn lower their academic performance. Aunola, 2000.

Baumrind also emphasized that parents' personal traits and characteristics are detrimental in child's development. So, apart from child's genetic predisposition, environmental aspects of prime importance in shaping overall psychological and social development which in turn is responsible for academic excellence. Form these social environmental factors positive parenting is considered key factor in stimulating child's learning trajectory. Still there are some myths that it is purely culture specific but when we review the cross-cultural literature the views remains consistently similar, that authoritative parenting is much more influencing that other kind of parenting styles. There is another kind of debatable issue that whether both the parents should be authoritative, one parent can be authoritative and other may choose to remain permissive or authoritarian as well. Baumrind (1991) has proponent of the thought the mother is considered more nurturing than controlling, and the father is usually more controlling than nurturing. So, the more fruitful combination of parenting style might be that father play as authoritative parent and mother as indulgent for development of progressive childhood. Simons, 2007 also, elaborated robustness of Authoritativeness by either parent, a combination of authoritativeness and indulgence, or even both the parents stay indulgent, child shows significantly better adjustment and achievement.

The child performance will remain worst in all arenas in case of an uninvolved mother with an indulgent or an uninvolved father. So, if the mother remains authoritative, chances of child's growth remain bleak and the chances remains bright when mother plays indulgent and father remains authoritative. Further if both mother and father are authoritarian there are high chances the child to lose self-confidence and poor decision making. The contributory discussion point is that the mother is responsible for the basic nurturance of the child and she should play the role of indulgent parent and father as controlling factor which promotes emotional stability and resilience.

Recently, I came across a case of conflicting situation between parents and their son in late twenties, where mother was play more like an authoritarian figure and father as uninvolved. The child was bright intellectually but few years back shows the signs of hopelessness and depression. He held the mother responsible for all his misery because he opined that he lost all his aspirations fulfilling mother's desire for academic excellence and could not enjoy life fully. Now, he don't want go to work and complains that nothing fruitful left in life. There are frequent in fights between family members, scapegoating each other. From a psychologist's perspective it is inferred to be a faulty case of parenting approach adopted by the family. The case could have been better if the mother remained indulgent and father as authoritative. It could have been normative even if at least both parents remained indulgent if not a pair of mother indulgent and father authoritative.

Aunola, K., Stattin, H.E., & Nurmi, J.E. (2000). Parenting styles and adolescents' achievement strategies. Journal of Adolescence, 23, 205-222.

Baumrind, D. (1966). Effects of authoritative parental control on child behaviour. Child Development, 37, 887–907.

Baumrind, D. (1991). Parenting styles and adolescent development. In J. Brooks-Gunn, R. Lerner, & A. C. Peterson (Eds.), The encyclopaedia of adolescence (pp.746-758). New York: Garland.

Simons, L. G., & Conger, R. D. (2007). Linking Mother-Father Differences in Parenting to a Typology of Family Parenting Styles and Adolescent Outcomes. Journal of Family Issues, 28(2), 212–241

Learning from Real-Life Experiences

The case studies and professional insights presented in this chapter offer a comprehensive view of the impact of helicopter parenting on both children and families. These real-life examples highlight the importance of finding a balance between being involved and giving children the space they need to grow into independent, confident adults.

Parents who recognize tendencies of helicopter parenting in themselves can take steps to adjust their approach, allowing their children to develop the skills they need to navigate life's challenges. By learning from the experiences of others and heeding the advice of professionals, parents can foster a healthier, more balanced parenting style that benefits both their children and themselves.

7. The Fine Line Between Involvement and Over Parenting

Balancing Support and Autonomy

Parenting is one of the most significant and challenging responsibilities in life. The love and care parents feel for their children often drive them to do everything possible to ensure their success and happiness. However, in the pursuit of providing the best for their children, some parents may find themselves overstepping boundaries, leading to what is commonly known as helicopter parenting. This chapter delves into the subtle yet crucial difference between healthy parental involvement and over parenting, emphasizing the importance of fostering independence in children while maintaining a supportive presence.

In many Indian families, the lines between support and control can often blur due to cultural expectations, societal pressures, and the natural desire to protect one's children from harm. Understanding these nuances is vital for parents who want to raise well-rounded, confident, and independent individuals. This chapter will guide you through recognizing the signs of over parenting, understanding the essence of healthy involvement, and adopting strategies that promote autonomy in children. You might feel better dealing in these issues after going through this chapter. And to be honest a lot of patience is required while trying to figure out the fine line between involvement and over parenting.

Healthy Parental Involvement: Understanding the Difference between Support and Control

Healthy parental involvement is rooted in the concept of balance. It's about being present in your child's life, offering guidance, and providing a safety net without overshadowing their ability to make decisions, face challenges, and learn from their experiences. This section explores what healthy involvement looks like and how parents can ensure they are not crossing into over parenting.

Open Communication: The Foundation of Healthy Involvement

One of the cornerstones of healthy parental involvement is open communication. In the Indian context, where respect for elders often means children are less vocal about their feelings, it's essential for parents to create an environment where their children feel safe expressing themselves. Open communication doesn't mean prying into every detail of your child's life; instead, it's about fostering an atmosphere where your child knows they can come to you with their thoughts, concerns, and decisions without fear of judgment or reprimand.

Encourage your child to share their day, talk about their challenges, and discuss their achievements. Listen actively, without interrupting or offering solutions right away. This practice helps build trust and ensures that your child feels valued and understood. For example, if your teenager is facing peer pressure, rather than dictating what they should do, engage in a conversation that allows them to explore their feelings and come to a decision they feel comfortable with.

Empathy and Understanding: Seeing the World through Their Eyes

Empathy is the ability to understand and share the feelings of another. In parenting, it means trying to see the world from your child's perspective. This approach helps you respond to their needs appropriately without imposing your expectations or fears. For instance, if your child is anxious about an upcoming exam, instead of dismissing their feelings or adding pressure, acknowledge their anxiety and offer support that empowers them, such as helping them create a study plan or practicing relaxation techniques.

Empathy also involves recognizing that your child's experiences and challenges are valid, even if they seem trivial to you. Whether it's a disagreement with a friend or stress over a minor school assignment, showing empathy allows your child to feel heard and supported which strengthens your relationship and builds their confidence.

Encouraging Independence: A Gradual Process

Encouraging independence is a gradual process that starts from a young age. It involves allowing your child to take on responsibilities, make decisions, and face the consequences of their actions. In India, where familial bonds are strong and parents often play a central role in their children's lives well into adulthood, fostering independence requires conscious effort.

Start by giving your child small tasks to complete on their own, such as choosing their clothes, packing their school bag, or helping with simple household chores. As they grow older, increase their responsibilities, encouraging them to manage their time, handle their schoolwork, and make decisions about extracurricular activities. This gradual increase in responsibility helps build their confidence and prepares them for the challenges of adult life.

Setting Boundaries: Knowing When to Step Back

While involvement is essential, it's equally important to set boundaries. Boundaries help your child understand that while you are there to support them, they also need to take responsibility for their actions. Setting boundaries means allowing your child to experience the natural consequences of their choices. For example, if your child chooses to procrastinate on their homework, let them face the consequences of receiving a lower grade rather than stepping in to complete the work for them.

Boundaries also apply to parents. It's important to recognize when your involvement is crossing into over control. This might mean resisting the urge to micromanage your child's schedule, avoid constantly checking up on them, or stepping back when they are capable of handling a situation on their own.

Offering Guidance, Not Solutions: Empowering Your Child

When faced with a problem, children often turn to their parents for advice. While it's tempting to solve the problem for them, offering guidance instead of solutions is more beneficial in the long run. This approach empowers your child to think critically, weigh their options, and come to their conclusions.

For instance, if your child is having trouble with a classmate, rather than telling them exactly what to do, ask questions that help them explore their feelings and consider different ways to handle the situation. This method not only helps them resolve the issue at hand but also teaches them problem-solving skills they will use throughout their lives.

Trusting Your Child: Building Confidence through Trust

Trust is a vital component of healthy involvement. Trusting your child means believing in their ability to make decisions and handle challenges. This doesn't mean you abandon your role as a guide and protector, but rather that you allow your child to take the lead when appropriate.

For example, trust your child to manage their study schedule for exams, to choose their friends, or to handle minor conflicts on their own. By showing trust, you help build their self-esteem and encourage them to develop the confidence needed to navigate the world independently.

Recognizing When Involvement Becomes Over parenting

Over parenting occurs when a parent's involvement crosses the line from supportive to controlling. This section discusses how to recognize the signs of over parenting and why it's important to avoid it.

Micromanaging Every Aspect of Your Child's Life

Micromanaging is one of the most common signs of over parenting. It involves controlling every detail of your child's life, from what they wear to who they befriend and how they spend their free time. This level of control can stifle your child's development and prevent them from learning how to make decisions and solve problems on their own.

For example, if you find yourself constantly organizing your child's activities, deciding what they should study, and even speaking on their behalf, it's time to step back. Allow your child to make their own choices, even if it means they might make mistakes. These mistakes are valuable learning experiences that help them grow.

Preventing Your Child from Facing Challenges

While it's natural to want to protect your child from pain and failure, shielding them from challenges can do more harm than good. Challenges and failures are an essential part of growth, teaching resilience, perseverance, and problem-solving skills.

If you find yourself constantly intervening to prevent your child from facing difficulties—whether by resolving conflicts for them, completing their tasks, or avoiding situations where they might struggle—you may be over parenting. Instead, encourage your child to face challenges head-on, offering support and guidance while allowing them to experience and learn from the outcomes.

Involvement in Every Detail of School and Social Life

Being overly involved in your child's academic and social life can lead to dependency and a lack of confidence. If you find yourself doing your child's homework, constantly communicating with their teachers, or arranging their social interactions, it's time to reassess your level of involvement.

Encourage your child to take responsibility for their schoolwork and social life. This might mean allowing them to organize their own study schedule, resolve conflicts with friends, or make decisions about their social activities. While it's important to be available for support, it's equally important to step back and let your child take the lead.

Constant Monitoring and Checking

Constantly monitoring your child's activities, whether through frequent check-ins, tracking their location, or insisting on constant updates, can undermine their sense of autonomy and trust. While it's important to be aware of your child's whereabouts and activities, excessive monitoring can create anxiety and dependency.

Trust your child to manage their time and responsibilities. Establish clear expectations and boundaries, but give them the space to navigate their daily life independently. This approach helps build trust and encourages your child to develop a sense of responsibility.

Struggling to Let Go

Over parenting often stems from a parent's difficulty in letting go. Whether it's due to fear, anxiety, or the desire to maintain control, this inability to step back can prevent your child from developing the independence they need.

Recognize that as your child grows, they need more freedom to make their own decisions and take responsibility for their actions. Letting go doesn't mean abandoning your role as a parent; it means allowing your child to grow into a self-sufficient individual while remaining a supportive and loving presence in their life.

Encouraging Independence: Strategies for Parents to Foster Autonomy

Encouraging independence in your child is not about withdrawing support but about equipping them with the tools and confidence to navigate the world on their own.

Start with Age-Appropriate Responsibilities

One of the best ways to encourage independence is to assign age-appropriate responsibilities. This approach helps children learn the value of contributing to their family and community while building their confidence and competence.

For younger children, responsibilities might include tasks like picking up toys, helping set the table, or choosing their clothes. As they grow older, these responsibilities can expand to include managing their homework, organizing their schedules, and helping with household chores. By gradually increasing the level of responsibility, you help your child develop the skills they need to manage their own life.

Encourage Problem-Solving: Building Critical Thinking Skills

Problem-solving is a crucial skill that children need to develop to become independent adults. When your child faces a challenge, resist the urge to step in and solve it for them. Instead, guide them through the problem-solving process.

Ask questions that encourage them to think critically about the issue, such as "What do you think are your options?" or "What could you do differently next time?" This approach helps your child learn to analyse situations, consider possible solutions, and make informed decisions.

Allow for Mistakes and Failures: The Value of Learning from Experience

Mistakes and failures are an inevitable part of life, and they offer valuable learning opportunities. Allowing your child to make mistakes and experience the consequences helps them develop resilience and learn how to cope with setbacks.

For example, if your child forgets their lunch at home, rather than rushing to deliver it to school let them experience the consequences of their forgetfulness. This experience will teach them to be more responsible in the future. While it's important to be supportive, it's equally important to let your child learn from their mistakes.

Encourage Decision-Making: Building Confidence and Responsibility

Decision-making is a critical skill that children need to develop to become independent. Encourage your child to make decisions from a young age, starting with simple choices like what to wear or what to eat. As they grow older, involve them in more significant decisions, such as planning their study schedule or choosing extracurricular activities.

When your child makes a decision, support them in following through, even if the outcome isn't perfect. This practice helps build their confidence and teaches them to take responsibility for their choices.

Model Independence: Leading by Example

Children learn a great deal by observing their parents. Model independence in your own life by demonstrating how you manage responsibilities, make decisions, and handle challenges. Show your child that it's okay to ask for help when needed, but also emphasize the importance of taking charge of one's own life.

For example, involve your child in everyday tasks like grocery shopping or budgeting, explaining how you make decisions and why. This not only teaches them practical skills but also shows them how to apply critical thinking to real-life situations.

Create a Supportive Environment: Balancing Guidance and Freedom

Encouraging independence doesn't mean leaving your child to figure everything out on their own. Create a supportive environment where they feel comfortable seeking advice and discussing their thoughts and feelings. Be there to guide them, but let them take the lead in finding solutions.

For instance, if your child is facing a difficult decision, such as choosing between two extracurricular activities, listen to their thoughts and ask open-ended questions to help them clarify their priorities. Offer insights based on your experience, but allow them to make the final decision.

Celebrate Independence and Effort: Positive Reinforcement

Positive reinforcement plays a crucial role in encouraging independence. Celebrate your child's efforts to be independent, even if the outcomes aren't always perfect. Praise their problem-solving skills, their willingness to take on responsibilities, and their ability to handle challenges.

For example, if your child takes the initiative to study for a test without being reminded, acknowledge their effort and discuss how their preparation might help them succeed. Celebrating their efforts rather than just the results reinforces the value of independence and perseverance.

Gradual Transition: Preparing for Greater Independence

As your child grows older, gradually transition more responsibilities to them, preparing them for the independence they will need in adulthood. This might include teaching them how to manage money, make decisions about their education and career, and handle personal relationships.

Discuss future plans with your child, helping them set goals and develop strategies to achieve them. Encourage them to take ownership of their decisions and actions, while remaining a supportive presence in their life.

Striking the Right Balance

Finding the right balance between involvement and independence in parenting is an on-going process that requires reflection, patience, and flexibility. It's about being there for your child when they need you while also giving them the space to grow, make mistakes, and learn from their experiences.

By understanding the difference between support and control, and by implementing strategies that foster autonomy, you can help your child develop the confidence and skills they need to thrive. Remember, your role as a parent is to guide and support your child, but also to trust them to navigate their own journey. By encouraging independence while remaining a source of love and guidance, you can help your child grow into a self-reliant, resilient individual ready to face the challenges of life with confidence.

8. Breaking the Cycle

The Need for Change

Parenting is a journey filled with love, challenges, and growth. For many parents, the desire to protect and guide their children can sometimes lead to over involvement, known as helicopter parenting. While the intentions behind this approach are often rooted in love and concern, the long-term effects can hinder a child's ability to develop independence, resilience, and problem-solving skills. Recognizing the need for change is the first step in breaking the cycle of helicopter parenting and moving toward a more balanced approach.

In this chapter, we will explore the importance of self-reflection for parents, offering tools and exercises to evaluate your behaviour and identify areas where change is needed. We will also provide practical steps for transitioning from helicopter parenting to a more balanced and supportive approach that fosters independence and confidence in your child.

Self-Reflection for Parents: Evaluating Your Behaviour

Self-reflection is a powerful tool for personal growth and change. It involves taking a step back to assess your actions, behaviours, and motivations as a parent. This process allows you to identify patterns of over parenting and understand the underlying reasons for these behaviours. Through self-reflection, you can gain insight into how your parenting style may be affecting your child and what changes are necessary to foster a healthier, more balanced relationship.

Understanding Your Parenting Motivations

One of the first steps in self-reflection is understanding why you parent the way you do. What drives your decisions and actions? Are they based on fear, anxiety, or the desire to control outcomes? Or are they rooted in a genuine desire to support your child's growth and independence?

Consider the following questions to help you reflect on your motivations:

- **What are your biggest fears for your child?** *Do these fears drive you to overprotect or over manage their life?*
- **How do you handle uncertainty or risk in your child's life?** *Do you find yourself trying to eliminate all risks, or are you comfortable with allowing your child to face challenges?*
- **What are your expectations for your child?** *Are these expectations realistic, or do they reflect your own desires and anxieties?*

By understanding your motivations, you can begin to identify areas where your behaviour may be more about your needs than your child's growth. This awareness is the first step toward making meaningful changes.

Identifying Patterns of Over parenting

The next step in self-reflection is to identify specific patterns of over parenting in your behaviour. This involves looking at how you interact with your child on a daily basis and recognizing situations where you may be overstepping boundaries.

Some common signs of over parenting include:

- **Micromanaging your child's schedule and activities.** *Do you plan every detail of their day, leaving little room for them to make decisions or explore their interests?*
- **Solving problems for your child.** *Do you often step in to resolve conflicts, complete tasks, or make decisions on their behalf?*
- **Constantly monitoring your child.** *Do you frequently check on your child's whereabouts, activities, and interactions, even when they are capable of managing these on their own?*
- **Avoiding or preventing challenges.** *Do you try to shield your child from difficulties, failures, or risks, rather than allowing them to learn from these experiences?*

Reflect on your daily interactions with your child and identify any patterns of over parenting. This self-awareness is essential for making changes and fostering a healthier, more balanced relationship.

Reflecting on the Impact of Your Behaviour

Once you've identified patterns of over parenting, it's important to reflect on how these behaviours may be affecting your child. Consider the following questions:

- How does your child respond to your involvement? *Do they seem anxious, dependent, or resistant to taking on responsibilities?*
- What skills is your child developing? *Are they learning to solve problems, make decisions, and handle challenges, or do they rely on you to manage these aspects of their life?*
- How is your relationship with your child? *Do they feel comfortable coming to you for guidance, or do they avoid sharing their thoughts and feelings?*

Reflecting on the impact of your behaviour helps you understand the consequences of over parenting and motivates you to make positive changes that support your child's growth.

Embracing Vulnerability and Imperfection

As parents, we often feel the need to be perfect and to have all the answers. However, embracing vulnerability and accepting that it's okay to make mistakes is a crucial part of self-reflection and growth. Recognize that parenting is a learning process, and it's normal to have moments of doubt, uncertainty, and imperfection.

Allow yourself to be vulnerable with your child, acknowledging when you've made a mistake or overstepped boundaries. This openness not only strengthens your relationship but also models humility and resilience for your child.

Practical Steps for Change: Transitioning to a Balanced Approach

Transitioning from helicopter parenting to a more balanced approach requires intentional effort and a willingness to change. The following steps offer practical strategies to help you make this transition while maintaining a supportive and loving presence in your child's life.

Gradual Release of Control: Allowing Your Child to Take the Lead

One of the most effective ways to transition from over parenting is to gradually release control and allow your child to take the lead in certain areas of their life. This process involves stepping back and giving your child the space to make decisions, solve problems, and take on responsibilities.

Start by identifying areas where your child is capable of handling tasks on their own. This might include managing their homework, organizing their schedule, or making decisions about extracurricular activities. Gradually increase their responsibilities as they demonstrate competence and confidence.

For example, if you've been closely managing your child's study schedule, begin by allowing them to create their own plan, offering guidance only when necessary. Encourage them to take ownership of their responsibilities and trust them to follow through.

Encouraging Independent Problem-Solving: Building Confidence and Resilience

Encouraging your child to solve problems independently is a key step in fostering their confidence and resilience. Instead of stepping in to resolve conflicts or complete tasks for them, guide them through the problem-solving process.

When your child encounters a challenge, ask open-ended questions that help them think critically about the situation. For example:

- **What options do you have in this situation?**
- **How do you think you should handle this problem?**
- **What might happen if you choose this option?**

By encouraging your child to explore different solutions and consider the consequences, you help them develop the skills they need to navigate challenges on their own.

Setting Boundaries for Yourself: Knowing When to Step Back

As a parent, it's important to set boundaries not just for your child, but also for yourself. Recognize when your involvement is crossing into over control and make a conscious effort to step back.

Establish clear boundaries around when and how you will intervene in your child's life. For example, decide that you will only step in when there is a serious issue or when your child specifically asks for help. This approach allows your child to take responsibility for their actions while still knowing that you are there to support them when needed.

Redefining Success: Focusing on Growth Rather Than Perfection

One of the reasons parents engage in helicopter parenting is the desire for their child to succeed and avoid failure. However, it's important to redefine success in terms of growth rather than perfection. Understand that mistakes and failures are valuable learning experiences that contribute to your child's development.

Encourage your child to take risks, try new things, and learn from their mistakes. Celebrate their efforts and progress, even if the outcome isn't perfect. By focusing on growth and resilience, you help your child develop a healthy attitude toward challenges and setbacks.

Seeking Support: Building a Network of Guidance

Transitioning from helicopter parenting to a balanced approach can be challenging, and it's important to seek support during this process. Reach out to other parents, educators, or counsellors who can offer guidance and share their experiences.

Consider joining parenting groups or attending workshops that focus on fostering independence and balanced involvement. Engaging with a supportive community can provide valuable insights and encouragement as you make changes in your parenting approach.

Implementing Self-Care: Taking Care of Your Well-Being

As you work on breaking the cycle of helicopter parenting, it's essential to prioritize your own well-being. Parenting can be stressful, and it's easy to become overwhelmed by the demands of raising a child. Implementing self-care practices helps you manage stress and maintain a healthy perspective.

Make time for activities that bring you joy and relaxation, whether it's exercising, spending time with friends, pursuing a hobby, or simply taking a moment for yourself. Taking care of your well-being not only benefits you but also sets a positive example for your child.

Communicating with Your Child: Building Trust and Understanding

As you transition to a more balanced approach, it's important to communicate openly with your child about the changes you're making. Explain why you're stepping back and encouraging them to take on more responsibilities. Emphasize that you trust their abilities and are confident in their capacity to handle challenges.

This communication helps build trust and understanding between you and your child. It also reinforces the idea that you are still there to support them, even as you encourage their independence.

Practicing Patience: Allowing Time for Growth

Change takes time, both for you and your child. As you work on breaking the cycle of helicopter parenting, it's important to practice patience. Understand that your child may need time to adjust to increased responsibilities and independence.

Be patient with yourself as well. Changing deeply ingrained habits and behaviours is a gradual process, and it's normal to experience setbacks along the way. Celebrate your progress and remain committed to fostering a healthier, more balanced relationship with your child.

Embracing a Balanced Parenting Approach

Breaking the cycle of helicopter parenting requires self-reflection, intentional effort, and a commitment to change. By understanding your motivations, identifying patterns of over parenting, and implementing practical strategies, you can transition to a more balanced approach that supports your child's growth and independence.

Remember, the goal is not to be perfect but to foster a healthy, supportive relationship with your child. By allowing them the space to explore, make mistakes, and develop their own identity, you help them build the confidence and resilience they need to thrive.

As you embrace a balanced parenting approach, you'll find that your child becomes more capable, self-reliant, and prepared to navigate the challenges of life. And in turn, you'll experience the fulfilment of watching your child grow into a confident, independent individual.

9. The Future of Parenting

A New Era of Parenting

As we stand on the threshold of an ever-changing world, the role of a parent is more challenging—and more crucial—than ever before. Our world is evolving at a dizzying pace, driven by technological advancements, shifting social norms, and global challenges that previous generations could hardly imagine. In this rapidly transforming landscape, parenting is no longer just about nurturing, educating, and guiding children through their early years. It's about preparing them for a future that is unpredictable, dynamic, and filled with opportunities and obstacles that we, as parents, must anticipate and navigate together.

The future of parenting promises to be as complex as it is exciting. The traditional models that once served families well may no longer suffice in the face of new realities. But within this uncertainty lies a powerful opportunity: the chance to redefine what it means to be a parent in the modern age. By embracing change, staying informed, and adapting our approaches, we can ensure that our children not only survive but thrive in the world they will inherit.

In this chapter, we'll explore the emerging trends in parenting, delve into the challenges that lie ahead, and discuss how we can prepare ourselves and our children for the future. This is not just about managing the present; it's about laying the foundation for a future where our children can flourish, no matter what comes their way.

The Digital Revolution: Parenting in the Age of Technology

It's impossible to discuss the future of parenting without acknowledging the profound impact of technology on our lives. From the moment they are born, today's children are immersed in a digital world. Tablets, smartphones, and the internet are as familiar to them as toys and books were to previous generations. This immersion in technology has transformed the way children learn, play, and interact with the world around them.

As parents, we are tasked with guiding our children through this digital landscape, which is filled with both promise and peril. On one hand, technology offers incredible educational tools, enabling children to access information and learns in ways that were unimaginable just a few decades ago. Online platforms can help children develop skills, explore their interests, and connect with others across the globe.

However, the digital world also presents significant challenges. Issues like screen addiction, cyber bullying, and exposure to inappropriate content are real concerns that parents must address. Moreover, the omnipresence of social media can impact a child's self-esteem and mental health, creating pressures that are difficult to manage.

In the future, the role of the parent will increasingly involve becoming digital mentors. We must stay informed about the latest technological trends, understand the platforms our children are using, and set boundaries that protect their well-being while allowing them to explore the digital world responsibly. This means having open conversations about the potential risks and rewards of technology, teaching children about online safety, and modelling balanced technology use ourselves.

It's also important to remember that while technology is a powerful tool, it should not replace real-world experiences and interactions. Parents must encourage children to engage in activities that promote creativity, physical health, and face-to-face communication. By fostering a healthy relationship with technology, we can help our children navigate the digital age with confidence and resilience.

Emotional Intelligence: The Key to Future Success

As the world becomes more complex, the skills that children need to succeed are also changing. While academic achievement and technical expertise will always be important, there is a growing recognition that emotional intelligence (EQ) is just as crucial, if not more so, for navigating the challenges of the future.

Emotional intelligence involves the ability to understand and manage one's own emotions, as well as the ability to empathize with others and build strong relationships. These skills are essential for success in a world where collaboration, communication, and adaptability are increasingly valued.

For parents, this means that nurturing emotional intelligence in children will become a central focus of our efforts. This involves more than just teaching children to manage their emotions; it's about helping them develop a deep understanding of themselves and others. By fostering empathy, self-awareness, and emotional regulation, we can prepare our children to handle the ups and downs of life with grace and resilience.

One way to cultivate emotional intelligence is through modelling. Children learn a great deal from observing how we, as parents, handle our own emotions and relationships. By demonstrating healthy emotional responses, effective communication, and conflict resolution, we provide our children with a blueprint for navigating their own emotional landscapes.

In addition to modelling, parents can create opportunities for children to practice emotional intelligence in their daily lives. This might involve encouraging them to express their feelings, guiding them through challenging social situations, or helping them reflect on their interactions with others. Activities such as journaling, role-playing, and discussing emotions in the context of stories or media can also be valuable tools for developing EQ.

As the future unfolds, emotional intelligence will likely play an even greater role in determining a child's success and well-being. By prioritizing this aspect of development, parents can give their children the tools they need to thrive in a world that values not just what they know, but how they connect with others.

Gender Equality: Raising a Generation without Limits

The conversation around gender has evolved significantly in recent years, and this evolution is poised to continue shaping the future of parenting. Traditional gender roles, which once dictated specific expectations for boys and girls, are being challenged and redefined. Today's parents are increasingly aware of the importance of raising children who feel free to explore their interests and talents, regardless of societal norms.

In the future, gender equality will likely become an even more integral part of parenting. This means fostering an environment where children can grow without being limited by stereotypes or expectations based on their gender. Parents will need to be vigilant in ensuring that their children have equal opportunities to explore different activities, express themselves freely, and develop a strong sense of identity.

Raising children in a gender-equal environment involves more than just providing equal opportunities; it's also about challenging the biases that can subtly influence a child's development. This might include questioning the messages children receive from media, toys, and even family members about what is "appropriate" for boys and girls. Parents can encourage their children to explore a wide range of activities, from sports to arts to STEM, and to pursue their passions without fear of judgment.

Furthermore, it's important to teach children about respect, consent, and the value of diversity from a young age. These lessons will help them grow into adults who not only understand gender equality but actively contribute to creating a more inclusive society.

As we look to the future, the role of parents in promoting gender equality will be critical. By raising a generation of children who are confident in their identities and respectful of others, we can help build a world where everyone has the opportunity to reach their full potential, regardless of gender.

Flexible Parenting: Adapting to Individual Needs

The future of parenting will likely see a shift away from rigid, one-size-fits-all approaches to more flexible and personalized parenting styles. As the understanding of child development deepens, it's becoming increasingly clear that each child is unique, with their own set of strengths, challenges, and needs.

In response to this, parents are beginning to adopt more adaptive approaches to parenting. Instead of following a strict set of rules or guidelines, they are tuning in to their child's individual personality, interests, and developmental stage, and adjusting their strategies accordingly.

This flexibility is not about abandoning structure or discipline, but rather about being responsive to the changing needs of a child. It's about recognizing that what works for one child may not work for another, and being willing to experiment with different techniques to find what works best for your family.

For example, some children may thrive with a lot of structure and routine, while others may need more freedom and flexibility to explore their interests. Some may require extra support in certain areas, while others may be more independent. By being attuned to these differences, parents can create an environment that supports each child's unique growth and development.

In the future, flexible parenting will likely become the norm as parents increasingly recognize the value of adapting their approaches to meet their children's individual needs. This trend reflects a broader shift toward a more personalized and child-cantered approach to parenting, where the focus is on helping each child reaches their full potential in a way that works for them.

The Challenge of Balancing Work and Family Life

As the boundaries between work and family life continue to blur, parents are facing new challenges in balancing their professional responsibilities with their roles as caregivers. The rise of remote work, the gig economy, and the increasing demands of modern careers are making it more difficult for parents to find the time and energy to be fully present with their children.

In the future, this challenge is likely to become even more pronounced, as technology enables greater connectivity and flexibility in the workplace, but also blurs the lines between work and personal life. Parents will need to be more intentional about setting boundaries and creating a balance that allows them to be fully engaged in both their work and their family life.

This might involve setting specific work hours, creating a dedicated workspace at home, and prioritizing family time in the evenings and on weekends. It will also be important to model a healthy work-life balance for children, teaching them the value of time management, self-care, and the importance of making time for the people and activities that matter most.

As workplaces evolve, parents may also need to advocate for policies that support work-life balance, such as flexible hours, parental leave, and access to childcare. By doing so, they can help create a more family-friendly work environment that benefits both parents and children.

Raising Global Citizens: Preparing Children for a Globalized World

The world is becoming increasingly interconnected, and today's children are growing up in a globalized society where they are exposed to different cultures, languages, and perspectives from a young age. The future of parenting will involve preparing children to thrive in this diverse and complex world.

This means fostering an appreciation for cultural diversity, teaching children to be open-minded and respectful of different viewpoints, and encouraging them to think critically about global issues. Parents can also expose their children to different cultures through travel, language learning, and interactions with people from diverse backgrounds.

Raising global citizens also involves instilling values of empathy, compassion, and social responsibility. By teaching children to care about the world beyond their immediate surroundings, parents can help them become active, engaged members of the global community.

As the world becomes more interconnected, the ability to understand and navigate different cultures will be an increasingly valuable skill. Parents who raise their children to be open-minded, empathetic, and globally aware will be giving them a powerful tool for success in the future.

The Impact of Climate Change: Raising Eco-Conscious Children

Climate change is one of the most pressing challenges of our time, and its impact will be felt by future generations. The future of parenting will involve preparing children to live in a world affected by environmental changes and encouraging them to be part of the solution.

Parents can start by educating their children about the importance of environmental stewardship and sustainability. This might involve teaching them about recycling, conservation, and the importance of reducing their carbon footprint. Parents can also model eco-friendly behaviours, such as reducing waste, conserving energy, and supporting sustainable practices.

In addition to these practical steps, parents can help their children develop the resilience and adaptability needed to cope with the uncertainties of climate change. This involves fostering a sense of hope and empowerment, encouraging children to be proactive in addressing environmental challenges, and supporting their involvement in initiatives that promote sustainability.

As climate change continues to impact our world, parents will play a crucial role in raising a generation that is informed, empowered, and committed to protecting the planet for future generations.

Embracing the Future with Confidence

The future of parenting is filled with both challenges and opportunities. As the world continues to evolve, so too must our approach to raising children. By staying informed about emerging trends, being adaptable in the face of new challenges, and prioritizing the well-being of our children, we can prepare them for the future with confidence.

Parenting in the modern world requires a delicate balance between guiding our children and giving them the freedom to explore and grow. It involves embracing change while holding on to the timeless values of love, support, and connection. As we look to the future, let us approach parenting with an open mind, a compassionate heart, and a commitment to helping our children thrive in an ever-changing world.

10. Resources and Further Reading

You're Not Alone on This Journey

Parenting is a journey filled with love, joy, challenges, and questions. As you navigate the complexities of raising your children, it's important to remember that you don't have to do it all on your own. Whether you're looking for guidance, support, or just a bit of reassurance, there are resources available to help you along the way.

In this chapter, we'll explore a variety of tools and resources that can provide you with valuable insights, practical advice, and emotional support. From books and articles to online communities and professional services, these resources are designed to empower you as a parent and help you create a nurturing environment for your children.

Articles: Bite-Sized Insights for Busy Parents

For parents who prefer quick reads or are looking for specific advice on particular issues, articles can be a great resource. The internet is full of valuable content, but here are some websites that consistently provide quality articles on parenting:

1. **ParentCircle**
   An Indian website that offers a wide range of articles on parenting, education, health, and family dynamics. ParentCircle is a go-to resource for practical tips and expert advice tailored to Indian families.

2. **The Swaddle**

   This online publication offers thoughtful articles on parenting, health, and culture. It's especially known for its nuanced takes on modern parenting challenges and its focus on raising children in today's world.

3. **YourDost**

   An online mental health and emotional wellness platform that provides articles on parenting, stress management, and relationships. It's particularly useful for parents who want to focus on their own mental well-being while raising their children.

4. **Times of India Parenting Section**

   As one of India's leading newspapers, the Times of India offers a dedicated parenting section with articles on everything from child development to parenting trends in India. It's a great resource for staying informed and getting practical advice.

Websites and Online Communities: Connect and Learn

In today's digital age, online communities and websites provide a space where parents can connect, share experiences, and seek advice. These platforms offer a wealth of information and the opportunity to engage with other parents who are going through similar experiences.

1. **BabyCenter India**

    This website offers a comprehensive range of resources, from pregnancy to parenting. It includes expert advice, interactive tools, and a community forum where parents can ask questions and share their stories.

2. **Parenting Nation**

    An Indian website that covers all aspects of parenting, from newborn care to teenage issues. It also features a forum where parents can connect and discuss various topics.

3. **Momspresso**

    A platform that caters to Indian mothers, offering blogs, articles, and videos on parenting, health, and lifestyle. It's a great place to find relatable content and connect with other moms.

4. **The Parent-Teacher Association (PTA) Groups on WhatsApp and Facebook**

    Many schools have PTA groups on social media where parents can connect, share information, and support each other. Joining these groups can help you stay informed about school activities and connect with other parents in your community.

Support Groups: Finding Your Tribe

Sometimes, the best support comes from connecting with other parents who understand what you're going through. Support groups, whether in person or online, provide a safe space where you can share your experiences, ask questions, and find comfort in knowing you're not alone.

1. **La Leche League India**

   For parents of newborns, La Leche League offers support and information on breastfeeding. They have local chapters across India and also provide online support through their website.

2. **Parent Support Groups on Facebook**

   Facebook hosts a variety of support groups for Indian parents. Whether you're looking for advice on specific parenting challenges or just want to connect with other parents, these groups can be a valuable resource.

3. **Local Parenting Meetups**

   Many cities in India have local parenting groups that organize meetups and events. These gatherings are a great way to meet other parents, share experiences, and build a support network.

4. **Nayi Disha Resource Centre**

   For parents of children with special needs, the Nayi Disha Resource Centre offers support, information, and resources. They provide a platform where parents can connect and share their journeys.

Professional Help: When You Need Extra Support

There may be times when you need more than just advice from books or articles. Professional help, whether from a counselor, psychologist, or parenting coach, can provide personalized guidance and support. Here are some options available to Indian parents:

1. **Child Psychologists and Counsellors**

   If you're concerned about your child's emotional or behavioural development, consulting a child psychologist or counsellor can be incredibly helpful. These professionals can offer insights into your child's needs and help you develop strategies for supporting them.

2. **Parenting Coaches**

   Parenting coaches provide personalized advice and support for parents looking to improve their parenting skills or navigate specific challenges. They can work with you to create a parenting plan that aligns with your family's values and goals.

3. **Online Counselling Services**

   Platforms like YourDost and BetterLyf offer online counselling services that allow you to connect with mental health professionals from the comfort of your home. This can be especially convenient for busy parents who need support but struggle to find the time for in-person appointments.

4. ## School Counsellors

Many schools in India now have counsellors on staff that can provide support to both students and parents. If you're concerned about your child's academic performance, social interactions, or emotional well-being, reaching out to the school counsellor can be a good first step.

Empowering Yourself with Knowledge and Support

Parenting is a lifelong journey, and like any journey, it's easier when you have the right tools and support. By exploring the resources available to you—whether they come in the form of books, articles, online communities, or professional help—you can equip yourself with the knowledge and confidence you need to navigate the challenges of parenting.

Remember, there's no one-size-fits-all approach to raising children. Every family is unique, and what works for one may not work for another. The key is to stay informed, remain open to learning, and seek support when you need it. With the right resources at your fingertips, you can create a loving, supportive environment where your children can thrive.

11. Finding Balance

The Importance of Balance

As we wrap up our exploration of parenting, one central theme has emerged: balance. The journey of raising children is not about achieving perfection but finding a harmonious middle ground where both parents and children can thrive. Balance is the cornerstone of effective parenting—it's about harmonizing involvement with independence, guidance with freedom, and support with self-reliance.

In today's fast-paced world, where societal pressures and external expectations can often overwhelm us, maintaining this balance can be challenging. We may feel tempted to micromanage every aspect of our children's lives in an effort to shield them from failure or ensure their success. Yet, the truth is that over parenting can inadvertently hinder their development, robbing them of the opportunities to learn from their experiences and grow resilient.

The essence of balanced parenting lies in understanding that while we play a crucial role in guiding and supporting our children, we must also step back and allow them the space to develop their own skills and independence. This means being present and attentive, yet also allowing our children to navigate challenges, make mistakes, and discover their own path.

Balance also involves taking care of ourselves as parents. It's about recognizing that our well-being directly impacts our ability to parent effectively. By managing stress, setting boundaries, and finding time for self-care, we can model a balanced approach for our children and ensure that we are at our best to support them.

Encouraging Healthy Development

The ultimate goal of parenting is to raise children who are well-adjusted, independent, and capable of navigating the complexities of the world with confidence and resilience. As we strive for this goal, it's important to keep a few key principles in mind:

Foster Independence: *Encourage your children to take on responsibilities and make decisions appropriate for their age. Allow them to experience the natural consequences of their actions, which help build problem-solving skills and self-confidence.*

Promote Emotional Resilience: *Equip your children with the tools to manage their emotions and cope with stress. Validate their feelings, teach them strategies for emotional regulation, and support them in developing a positive mind-set.*

Support Self-Discovery: *Give your children the freedom to explore their interests and passions. Provide opportunities for them to engage in various activities, and encourage them to pursue their unique talents and dreams.*

Cultivate Strong Relationships: *Build a foundation of trust and open communication within your family. Show your children that they are loved and* *valued, and create an environment where they feel comfortable sharing their thoughts and feelings.*

Model Balanced Living: *Demonstrate the principles of balance in your own life. Practice self-care, manage your own stress effectively, and model healthy behaviours. Your actions will serve as a powerful example for your children.*

Encourage Lifelong Learning: *Foster a love for learning and curiosity in your children. Support their education and personal growth, and encourage them to embrace new experiences and challenges.*

By focusing on these principles, you can help your children develop into well-rounded individuals who are prepared to face the world with confidence and resilience. Remember, parenting is a journey filled with ups and downs, and finding balance is an on-going process. There will be times when you need to adjust your approach, reflect on your strategies, and seek support. But through it all, maintaining a balanced perspective will help you navigate the complexities of parenting and raise children who are capable, compassionate, and confident.

In the end, parenting is not about achieving a perfect outcome but about striving to provide a nurturing and supportive environment where your children can flourish. By embracing the principles of balance and focusing on healthy development, you are giving your children the greatest gift of all—a foundation for a happy, fulfilling, and successful life.

Happy Parenting, Happy Living!!

Bibliography

Books

1. **Chua, Amy.** *Battle Hymn of the Tiger Mother.* *Penguin Books, 2011.*
   - *This book offers insight into the intense parenting style often associated with Asian cultures, providing a perspective on helicopter parenting.*
2. **Faber, Adele, and Mazlish, Elaine.** *How to Talk So Kids Will Listen & Listen So Kids Will Talk.* *Scribner, 2012.*
   - *A classic book on effective communication strategies between parents and children.*
3. **Greene, Ross W.** *Raising Human Beings: Creating a Collaborative Partnership with Your Child. Scribner, 2016.*
   - *Focuses on collaborative solutions and understanding a child's unique needs to reduce conflict.*
4. **Tsabary, Shefali.** *The Parenting Map: A Complete Guide to Raising Emotionally Intelligent Children. Penguin Life, 2021.*
   - *Offers practical tools for conscious parenting and connecting with children on a deeper level.*

Articles

1. *"Parenting Nation." Parenting Nation, www.parentingnation.in.*

- Provides a range of articles on parenting, education, and family dynamics relevant to Indian families.
2. **"The Swaddle."** *The Swaddle,* *www.theswaddle.com.*
   - *Features thoughtful articles on modern parenting challenges and insights.*
3. **"YourDost."** *YourDost,* *www.yourdost.com.*
   - *Offers articles on parenting, mental well-being, and emotional support.*
4. **"Times of India Parenting Section."** *Times of India, www.timesofindia.indiatimes.com.*
   - *Provides articles and advice on various aspects of parenting in India.*

Websites and Online Communities

1. **BabyCenter India.** *BabyCenter India,* *www.babycenter.in.*
   - *Comprehensive resource for pregnancy and parenting information with interactive tools and community support.*
2. **Parenting Nation.** *Parenting Nation,* *www.parentingnation.in.*
   - *Covers all aspects of parenting and includes a forum for parent discussions.*
3. **Momspresso.** *Momspresso,* *www.momspresso.com.*
   - *Features blogs, articles, and videos on parenting and lifestyle from an Indian perspective.*
4. **Nayi Disha Resource Centre.** *Nayi Disha,* *www.nayidisha.org.*

    o *Provides support and resources for parents of children with special needs.*
5. **La Leche League India.** *La Leche League India, www.llli.org.*
    o *Offers breastfeeding support and resources for new parents.*
6. **Local Parenting Meetups.** *Information can be found through community boards and local parenting groups in your area.*

Support Groups and Professional Help

1. **YourDost.** *YourDost, www.yourdost.com.*
    o *Online platform providing mental health support and counselling services.*
2. **BetterLyf.** *BetterLyf, www.betterlyf.com.*
    o *Offers online counselling and emotional support services.*
3. **School Counsellors.** *Information on available counsellors can be obtained from local schools and educational institutions.*

Case Studies and Examples

- *The case studies and real-life examples referenced in this book were drawn from a range of sources, including anecdotal evidence from interviews with parents and children, as well as insights shared by professionals in the field of psychology, education, and counselling.*
- *Specific examples were provided through professional perspectives from psychologists and educators, including interviews and consultations with experts in child development and parenting.*

ChatGPT AI. *For paraphrasing and rephrasing few paragraphs in different sections.*

By drawing on these resources, this book aims to offer a comprehensive and practical guide to parenting that is informed by a wide range of expert opinions and real-world experiences.